LAND

D0802551

LAND

A NEW PARADIGM FOR A THRIVING WORLD

—

MARTIN ADAMS

North Atlantic Books
Berkeley, California

Copyright © 2015 by Martin Adams under a Creative Commons copyright (CC BY-NC-ND 3.0). For more information about this Creative Commons license, please visit: http://CreativeCommons.org.

North Atlantic Books
P.O. Box 12327
Berkeley, California 94712

Cover art: *San Francisco in July, 1849,* by George Henry Burgess
Cover and book design by Jasmine Hromjak
Printed in the United States of America

Land: A New Paradigm for a Thriving World is sponsored and published by the Society for the Study of Native Arts and Sciences (dba North Atlantic Books), an educational nonprofit based in Berkeley, California, that collaborates with partners to develop cross-cultural perspectives, nurture holistic views of art, science, the humanities, and healing, and seed personal and global transformation by publishing work on the relationship of body, spirit, and nature.

Neither the author nor the publisher of this work accept any liability for any investment or tax decisions made on the basis of the information contained herein; this work does not constitute financial or tax advice and should not be taken as such.

North Atlantic Books' publications are available through most bookstores. For further information, visit our website at www.northatlanticbooks.com or call 800-733-3000.

Library of Congress Cataloging-in-Publication Data

Adams, Martin, 1979-
  Land : a new paradigm for a thriving world / Martin Adams
      pages cm.—(Sharing the earth)
  Summary: "Sources the underlying causes of wealth inequality, social decline, and environmental destruction to the ownership of land as a basis for wealth"—Provided by publisher
   ISBN 978-1-58394-920-7 (paperback)—ISBN 978-1-58394-921-4 (ebook)
  1. Land use. 2. Wealth. 3. Sustainable development. 4. Equality. I. Title.
  HD156.A33 2014 333.3--dc23
                        2014032109

1 2 3 4 5 6 7 UNITED 18 17 16 15 14

Printed on recycled paper

To each of us, with love.

And to you, Peter ♥!

♡ Martin
3/24/2016

CONTENTS

ACKNOWLEDGMENTS

The conscious and dedicated actions of many people have made this work possible. First, there are those who influenced me in significant ways and who prepared me to conceive of this work. I would like to especially thank Logan Rose for reaffirming in me a vision of a humanity where everyone is fed, clothed, sheltered, and cared for, as well as for patiently mentoring me in many aspects of living. My gratitude also goes to Dan Millman, whose invaluable teachings have formed my character in significant ways and whose faith in me—both as a human being and as a writer—helped me trust in the value of what I have to share. Both Logan and Dan offered extensive feedback that helped make this work what it is today; I gratefully acknowledge both men as significant influences in my life and work. I also offer deep and abiding gratitude to my former partner Saskia, who painstakingly read through several drafts, shared illuminating insights, and offered helpful editing suggestions.

A group of friends paid close attention to both prose and content, and collaboratively reviewed, edited, and provided in-depth feedback for the manuscript. In particular, Daniel Syddall, Jacob Shwartz-Lucas, Jeffery J. Smith, Nate Blair, and Edward Miller contributed in major ways. Dan Sullivan, Chris and Dawn Agnos, Marina

Smerling, Justin Keith, Shane Powers, Rick Heggem, and Mickey Chaplan also provided additional feedback that helped clarify the message. Kelley Eskridge of Sterling Editing refined an earlier edition of this work, while Nancy Grimley Carleton did another extensive edit for the current edition—I'm exceptionally grateful to both for their outstanding work.

My heartfelt gratitude also to the entire team at North Atlantic Books, especially to Doug Reil and Tim McKee for seeing this work's potential, as well as to Louis Swaim for his project editing, Lauren Harrison for her careful copyediting, and Jasmine Hromjak for her book design. From my heart, a big thank you to all who have poured their labor and love into this work.

Fred Harrison influenced me during a critical stage in this book's development; I learned much from him over a relatively short period of time and continue to be grateful for the lessons I received. I would also like to thank Fred Foldvary for helping me better understand the material, for patiently taking time to answer my many questions, and for providing essential feedback during the early stages. Further acknowledgments go to Robin Smith, who communicated wisdom that provided the crucible for this work, as well as to the late Adrian Wrigley, whose land-use concept provides a groundbreaking solution. Thanks also to Chris Baulman, whose focus on land as a fundamental human right helped me gain an entirely new perspective on its value. I also extend my sincere gratitude to Susan

Taylor for her support and creative inspiration, especially in the early days when encouragement was much needed and hard to come by.

Since this work itself is chiefly based on the teachings of a number of economists and laypeople who have devoted their lives in service to the betterment of the human condition, I owe them a particular debt of gratitude for their piercing insights and eloquent explanations. Many of them work tirelessly—petitioning in city halls, educating in classrooms, blogging on the internet—to promote the economic ideas contained in this work, ideas that have the potential to truly and radically change our world.

No acknowledgment is complete without a heartfelt appreciation of the people who've left an indelible mark upon my life in ways both large and small: teachers, mentors, friends, relatives, and beloveds. You know who you are, and I'm grateful for your love and encouragement; I probably couldn't have written this work without your support along the winding path of life, offered silently or overtly, from afar or from up close. I offer a special acknowledgment to my mother, Heide, and my father, Günther: My mother's sacrifice and enduring support is to me forever a clarion call to love, and my father's compassion lives on inside my heart and in my memories; because of their inspiring examples, I'm able to do my small part in the greater scheme of things. I thank them both from the bottom of my heart.

And last, and most of all, I bow to the ever-present, silent Reality that abides both within and without for the unconditional love it inspires and the infinite Grace it forever bestows.

INTRODUCTION

Like slavery and apartheid, poverty is not natural. It is man-made and it can be overcome and eradicated by the actions of human beings.

—Nelson Mandela (1918–2013)

Everyone has a place in this world, and we all deserve to be able to meet our basic needs. There's enough material wealth on the planet to allow every human being to live a dignified life that fulfills our individual and collective needs and potentials. But we each require access to material resources—not only to meet our basic needs but also to support our higher needs for self-expression and self-actualization. Except for the privileged few, however, most of us don't have enough money and resources to live free of want and to fully serve whatever higher cause may call us.

Take a look around you, in whatever environment you find yourself right now. Unless you're in nature, most of what you see was created by at least one other human being. In fact, almost *everything* in our daily lives connects us to actions performed by other people—past actions that leave anonymous footprints on our lives today. We do indeed live in a world of our own making; we mold our shared environment to reflect our collective imagination. Together we create the shapes and forms that influence our perceptions and inform our daily thinking. This reality holds true for the small things in life, like objects of furniture, up to the larger things, such as social structures, systems of commerce, and even types of government. We have created all of these things and more.

Whatever we can create, we can also modify, take apart, and re-create. It's critically important that we acknowledge this truth when we consider our current social and economic systems: They exist not by default but because we created them, and they will continue to exist as long as most of us choose, consciously or unconsciously, to uphold them in their current forms. They are, in a real and practical sense, a direct outgrowth of our collective thoughts and actions.

Collective is an important word here: The effects of our choices and actions ripple throughout other people's lives and leave subtle imprints upon our individual consciousness as well. We have all experienced this truth: For example, acts of kindness can offer us the experience of what it feels like to be kind, while acts of dishonesty can give us the experience of what it feels like to be cut off from an authentic connection with other people. Every act comes with swift consequences to ourselves, as well as to others.

Our actions are very often guided by the economic systems we live in because such systems reward or discourage certain kinds of behaviors with various economic incentives that are constantly created through the web of laws, customs, habits, and agreements that define these systems. These external incentive structures may or may not always encourage us to act in service to a greater good, and thereby, ultimately, to serve ourselves. If we want to encourage behavior that benefits us on a material as well as on a psychological level, we need to modify the economic incentive structures we have created so that they better reflect the reality of our interconnectedness.

Most of us are familiar with the game of Monopoly, in which players build houses and hotels on the parcels they own and collect increasing amounts of rent whenever other players land on these parcels. Because the game limits the available number of real-estate parcels, the player able to buy the most real estate, through either sheer luck or shrewd deal making—or usually a combination— commands the highest rents and wins the game by driving the other players into bankruptcy.

It turns out that we're all playing a real-life version of Monopoly, and this game profoundly shapes our lives at every moment. However, in contrast to the board game, we don't experience our real-life losses through heated debates around the kitchen table; rather, we may experience them as the despair of being unable to sufficiently provide for ourselves, despite our willingness to do so. To compound matters, we're far along in this game: All available real-estate parcels have been bought, houses and hotels have been constructed, and those of us who are less fortunate are faced with great, often insurmountable, obstacles. In all too many cases, people with low incomes can't meet even their basic needs without governmental assistance, despite their desire to work and contribute to society and despite the massive amount of wealth that's already present in the economy. Worse yet, in many places around the world, governments are unwilling or unable to provide that basic assistance. Meanwhile, upward mobility has become unattainable for many, particularly for those who have little to start with.

Most of us wish to live in a society that encourages fairness and makes it possible for people of all socioeconomic levels to bring about their own success. One of our cultural myths in the West tells us that we live in a meritocracy, a society that rewards each person financially in direct proportion to the tangible value he or she provides to that society—that is, in direct accordance to that person's talents and work ethic, and regardless of gender, class, race, or other attributes. But the fact is that many of us work hard and are tremendously skilled at what we do, but receive only a paltry reward for our labor, while those born into wealth, for example, are spared from the need to work or contribute in any way. Our current economic system doesn't compensate human beings for much of the value they create for society, while many individuals receive substantial amounts of unearned wealth from other people's efforts.

The only way we can ensure fair and enduring prosperity for every member of our society is to reshape our economy from *the ground up*, which means that we need to address and solve the underlying disparities at the root level. Whether we're talking about the destruction of nature, urban sprawl, unemployment, crime, wealth inequality, or even war, the root cause is the simple fact that, despite our cultural and technological sophistication, we haven't yet learned to share with one another the most basic element that needs to be shared with all: the ground upon which we walk. Land. By allowing some people to profit from land, we have privatized community wealth, which allows a few to live off the lives of the rest of us.

In the first part of *Land*, I'll discuss how wealth is produced and how this production adds value to both individual producers and consumers, as well as to society. Next, I'll review how individuals and institutions profit from land at the expense of society and how this process causes wealth inequality, unemployment, economic recessions, and ecological destruction. From there, I'll examine what it means to live materially and culturally in harmony with the greater web of life. Throughout, I've done my best to boil the concepts down to the basics; those who are interested in the more technical details can consult the endnotes and appendix.

The second part of the book describes a time-tested economic theory most recently repopularized in the eighteenth and nineteenth centuries when notable economists and thinkers such as David Ricardo, John Stuart Mill, Henry George, and many others rediscovered and contributed significantly to this theory. Adam Smith, one of history's best-known economists, spoke of it in his 1776 magnum opus, *An Inquiry into the Nature and Causes of the Wealth of Nations.* Today, this theory is discussed with great sophistication by a wide range of economists who have devoted their lives to the betterment of humankind, with the understanding that the problems we currently face *can* be solved at the most fundamental level. In this part of the book, I again boil these concepts down to their basics, with the hope that they will help guide readers on what steps to take to create a new paradigm for a thriving world.

Let's imagine a world where both lighthearted play and purposeful work, not drudgery, are the order of the day for all human beings—a world where our reality overflows with material abundance and where everyone can focus on maximizing their potential instead of on scrounging for money. My greatest hope is that one day each human being—every one of us—will be able to participate in a society that's inherently just and that also considers the well-being of future generations. To achieve this, we have to work together in appreciation of our differences and on behalf of our common humanity. When enough of us work together for the common good, then, to paraphrase Buckminster Fuller, we will one day create a world that works for everyone.

Martin Adams
Fall 2014
Middletown, California

PART I: THE COST OF IGNORANCE

The first man who, having enclosed a piece of land, ventured to say, "This is mine" and found people simple enough to believe him was the real founder of civil society. How many crimes, wars, murders, how many miseries and horrors might the human race have been spared by the one who, pulling up the stakes or filling in the ditch, had shouted to his fellow men: "Beware of listening to this impostor; you are lost if you forget that the fruits of the Earth belong to all and that the Earth belongs to no one."

—Jean-Jacques Rousseau (1712–1778)

1. THE PRODUCTION OF WEALTH

I am sure that each of you would want to go beyond the superficial social analyst who looks merely at effects and does not grapple with underlying causes. True compassion is more than flinging a coin to a beggar; it understands that an edifice which produces beggars needs restructuring.

—Martin Luther King Jr. (1929–1968)

The late publisher Alfred A. Knopf once quipped, "An economist is a man who states the obvious in terms of the incomprehensible." But the subject of economics doesn't have to be incomprehensible; since all economic principles are grounded in human behavior, you really need only your common sense to understand them. Indeed, if we're ever to create a world where we can all enjoy materially fulfilling and dignified lives while also living in harmony with nature, it's *vital* that we properly understand economics, because the science of economics underlies the study of social welfare.

Let's begin with an initial overview of economics that may at first seem abstract, but which has relevant and practical applications in subsequent chapters. If a concept isn't clear to you at first, it will become clearer upon further reading, since we'll look at our central thesis from different angles throughout this book. Our main interest here is the basics;

if you're interested in some of the more technical aspects, you may also wish to consult the endnotes and appendix.

In this book, we'll define *economic wealth* as all goods and services that can be perceived with our senses, that are produced with human effort or the use of machinery, that directly satisfy human desires, and that have an exchange value. This particular definition is important because a conventional understanding of wealth isn't precise enough for our purposes. One key example: Under our definition, money isn't *economic wealth*, since it can't satisfy human desire directly, but only indirectly when we exchange it for something else (a person stranded on a deserted island quickly realizes that money itself isn't real wealth). Nature's gifts such as fresh air, water, and land are also not economic wealth, because no human being has made them. Under our definition, human-made goods and services are economic wealth because goods and services can add value to our lives. So, when we talk about how wealth is created, it's important to keep in mind our specific definition of *economic* wealth; whenever I use the term *wealth*, I mean *economic wealth* as defined here.[1]

On the most foundational level, wealth is created from nature, human labor, and tools. The so-called classical economists of the eighteenth and nineteenth centuries referred to these three elements as the three *factors of production*: *land*, *labor*, and *capital*. The term *land* refers to all gifts of nature; the term *labor* to human effort; and the term *capital* to capital goods such as tools and machinery.

Under this definition, *land* refers not simply to parcels of land, but to anything freely provided by nature, including the air, minerals, trees, and water, and even the electromagnetic spectrum.[2]

The term *labor* is pretty straightforward and signifies all human exertion, both mental and physical, aimed toward the production of wealth.

The term *capital* means all previously created wealth that's put toward the creation of new wealth. The word *capital* here doesn't mean money, but rather refers to capital goods: human-made objects such as machines or buildings that assist in the production of new wealth. Over time, we generally produce more wealth than we consume or destroy, and so our societies have a surplus of capital goods; everywhere we look, we see factories, office buildings, computers, trucks, and railroads, all standing by and ready to assist humanity in the production of new wealth.

Broadly speaking, there are only two ways human beings can make an income: They can either make an income by contributing to society, or they can extract an income from society.[3] People can contribute to society by providing valuable goods and services: When human beings add value to the wealth production process through their labor, that added value can be classified as a wage (for example, when a mechanic buys a car, repairs it, and then sells it for more money afterward, that sales differential becomes her wage); and when capital goods add value to the wealth production process, that added value is what economists call a capital return (for example, the value added by the mechanic's use of time-saving power tools is a return on the mechanic's capital—her power tools).[4]

The only other way people can make an income is by receiving what economists call *economic rent*. They do this not by adding wealth to society, but by extracting an income from society without providing wealth of corresponding value. For example, when people make money from selling land, they extract economic rent from society since they didn't contribute any human-made wealth to society.[5]

The problem with rent extraction is that the more rent people extract from society, the fewer resources remain to pay people for their goods and services. Because many people extract economic rent from society on an ongoing basis, the people who add value to society—employees, small business owners, independent contractors, and so forth—are left with a much smaller share of the economic pie from which to draw an income.

We'll return to these concepts in different ways throughout the following chapters. The important thing to remember is that wealth production utilizes nature's gifts, human labor, and tools, and that we can either get paid for providing goods and services that add value to society, or simply extract money without creating any corresponding value for society. Now that we've looked at and clarified these economic principles, the stage is set for us to explore how land attains its value.

2. THE VALUE OF LOCATION

What is there in our economic life more significant than the fact that a majority must pay the relatively few for the privilege of living and of working on those parts of the surface of the Earth which geological forces and community development have made desirable?

—Harry Gunnison Brown (1880–1975)

In order to better understand how we can transition to a more equitable and thriving society, we turn to another fundamental: Due to its inherently limited supply for each location, land obtains its value from the natural, social, and cultural wealth that exists in its surrounding environment. The convenience of being able to partake in all of the goods and services available in a particular location manifests in higher land values for that particular location. For example, people can access more goods and services on urban land than on rural land due to urban land's *locational* advantage, but this locational advantage arises only as a result of the additional wealth that exists in the surrounding environment—wealth that people have created in cooperation and in competition with one another. This principle is known as the *Law of Rent*.[6] The *Law of Rent* is as universal as the law of gravity, and as central to the human experience. Just like gravity, it affects us at all times; like gravity, it can't be seen with the naked eye, and most of us take it for granted. The real-estate maxim "Location, location, location" is grounded in the Law of Rent.[7]

MEDIA 2-1: THE LAW OF RENT

A simple explanation of the Law of Rent.
http://unitism.co/lawofrentstory

If we look deeply at life, we realize that the benefits we receive from society are largely attributable to their location. Benefits are *local* to the areas that we live in: the roads we drive on, the stores we shop at, and the services we use. These benefits are convenient to us because of their proximity, and the *land* upon which these conveniences exist enables their existence. In fact, the more conveniences exist in a general area, the more valuable the area's land becomes.

The Law of Rent affects *everything*. This concept is so basic and yet so profound that, once properly understood, it has the potential to forever change the way we view the world. The Law of Rent demonstrates that no single human being gives land and location its overall value—its *rent*. Land values arise from the wealth that exists in the surrounding area, wealth that we have created together and continue to create in cooperation and in competition with one another. Land values, as we shall see, are financial reflections of our interconnectedness.

8

3. THE FREE MARKET

Neither social justice nor a well-functioning free market system can long be enjoyed without the other.

—Kris Feder,
Associate Professor of Economics,
Bard College

A truly free market is a healthy component of any balanced society. Markets are free when human beings have equal opportunities to influence the production and trade of desirable goods and services. When people compete to produce goods or services, some are able to attain market control and set market prices due to favorable natural, social, or political conditions: They attain a monopoly. The problem with monopolies, however, is that they enable those who have attained them to extract money from society without providing goods or services of corresponding value.[8]

When a single entity has complete control over a market, this is known as an *absolute monopoly*. But monopolies can also occur when the market is simply closed to new participants because overall supply can't be increased; these are known as *entry monopolies* because outside entities are unable to participate in the market unless another entity that's *already* participating in the market is willing to transfer its market privileges to the outside entity.

The market for top-level internet domains—those ending in ".com" or ".org," for example—is an entry monopoly. Because actual domain names can't be replicated (for example, there can't be another progress.org) and because there are only a limited number of sensible letter combinations, the market for top-level internet domain names today is no longer a free market, but rather a *monopolized market*. As many people who want to register internet domains know, many good domain names are already owned by individuals and companies that don't actually put them to productive use, but rather control the names solely in order to resell them at exorbitant prices.

Land ownership is also an entry monopoly: Land is naturally scarce for each location since its supply can't be increased. New land can't be created, so if people wish to become landowners, they have to buy land from someone who already owns it. The perspective that the ownership of land is an entry monopoly may seem strange at first because few of us are taught to view the real-estate market in this light. But let's examine the issue from another perspective: How much does it cost to produce land? Nothing, because land can't be produced, yet people make money from land nonetheless. The real-estate market in land has to be a monopoly since, per our previous definition, monopolies allow participants to extract money from society without providing human-made goods or services of corresponding value.

Real-estate agents, small business owners, and property managers know only too well that *location* gives a particular piece of land, or property, a competitive advantage over another. A rundown house in an expensive neighborhood tends to be more valuable than an expensive house of similar size in a rundown neighborhood. Why? Because the desirable social qualities that exist in a location give land its value, and those qualities can't be unilaterally created by the property owners themselves; the desirable qualities can only be gained from the wealth, convenience, and benefits that exist in the surrounding environment.

This locational advantage, afforded through the monopolistic nature of the market, allows property owners to profit from land. When people buy a piece of land, their ownership gives them the right to exclude the rest of society from the benefits afforded to them by *their* land, even though those benefits only arise from nature and from the presence of goods and services that have been provided by that same society in the first place. Buyers pay for *exclusive access rights* to land and pay only to the previous landowner instead of to all the people who are now excluded from the location privileges that this one particular piece of land provides; although these excluded people could live elsewhere, similar entry monopolies are in place elsewhere as well. We live in an economic system that allows a single buyer to own a part of the Earth without requiring the owner to reimburse those negatively affected by their exclusion.

Let's imagine that we own an empty plot of land. We could lease it out on the open market to someone else for

$6,000 per year, or, alternatively, put it to use ourselves. Its annual market value of $6,000 is the value that other individuals are willing to pay in order to obtain access to the advantages that this particular land in this particular location provides: In other words, this figure gives us the land's *rent*. Let's hire a part-time farmer for $9,000 to operate a small farm on this piece of land, and let's also purchase equipment for $3,000. Let's assume that by the end of the season, the farm will have produced $20,000 worth of produce (table 3-1).

TABLE 3-1: FARM PROFIT

Land (rent)	$	(6,000)
Farmer (wages)	$	(9,000)
Machinery (capital)	$	(3,000)
Total expenses	**$**	**(18,000)**
Farm produce	$	20,000
Rent	$	6,000
Revenues	**$**	**26,000**
Gross Profit	**$**	**8,000**

We know that the rental value of the land we own—how much *other* people would pay for the privilege to use the land had they the opportunity to do so—is $6,000 a year. But because we own the land and thus are in a monopoly

12

position, we can pay the cost of $6,000 to ourselves.[9] As property owners we gain an extra $6,000 in benefits through our ownership of land. While this resource is *withheld* from the market, the market itself is not compensated for its exclusion, and so the market is artificially restricted. And even though we as landowners may pay a fair market value for our land at the time of purchase, we only pay this purchase price to another individual—the previous property owner—and *not to all the market participants who have been excluded.*

In theory, capitalism is an economic system that allows people to freely trade goods and services in a competitive free market. But since the outright ownership of land creates an entry monopoly, it restricts the operation of the free market. By falsely believing that our markets are free, we've created a misunderstanding of historical proportions. Capitalism has prided itself on the efficiency of the free market system for centuries, but because capitalism allows people to monopolize land and other gifts of nature, we need to realize that we may have never had *true capitalism* in the sense that the markets have never been *truly free.* However, because of this misunderstanding, many of us tend to look upon capitalism—or at least what passes for capitalism— with great disdain. And appropriately so: Our current implementation of capitalism is deeply responsible for the exploitation of nature and the decline of social well-being.

The mistaken belief that markets are free when their freedom is, in fact, inhibited by monopolistic behavior is one of the primary sources of economic suffering in the world today. But our current implementation of capitalism is not the only economic system that produces suffering. Let's consider other economic systems. *Communism*, for example, is a system in which the means of production are owned and controlled by the state; it advocates the elimination of private-wealth production altogether. *Socialism*, meanwhile, is somewhere between capitalism and communism. Both capitalism and socialism allow individuals to be compensated for their goods and services, but they also allow individuals to monopolize land; communism, on the other hand, points to people's ability to make money from wealth production as one of the root causes of economic dysfunction, and thus collectivizes the wealth-production process altogether. All three systems fail to remedy a whole range of public and social issues because they fail to understand the mechanisms by which private parties extract rent from society by monopolizing land and how this extraction harms society.[10]

Many property owners and financial institutions making money from mortgage-backed securities currently profit from land similarly to the way slave owners profit from the labor of slaves. Without the institution of slavery, slave owners would have to hire workers in a competitive labor market. Similarly, the duty-free ownership of land allows property owners—and financial institutions that finance property ownership—to obtain unearned benefits from land; were this not the case, property owners would have to compete for the value provided by land on a rental or leasing basis. Horace Greeley, journalist and fervent abolitionist at a time when slavery was still legal in many parts of America, observed that "whenever the ownership of the soil is so engrossed by a small part of the community that the far larger part are compelled to pay whatever the few may see fit to exact for the privilege of occupying and cultivating the earth, there is something very much akin to slavery."

One of the main reasons we have thus far not had much public discussion about the ability of individuals to profit from land is that *most economists treat nature as capital!* They treat land and all other gifts of nature as capital, despite the fact that land is nonproducible and has a limited supply for each location, whereas capital is a result of human production. This failure to distinguish land from capital prevents economists from recognizing the monopoly that allows people to extract incomes from society.

Economists Mason Gaffney and Fred Harrison claim in their work *The Corruption of Economics*, first published in 1994, that industrialists toward the end of the nineteenth century may have intentionally created and promoted a new brand of economics to divert public attention from the monopolization of nature.[11] Gaffney and Harrison's work takes a fresh look at how the original science of economics was deliberately and increasingly sidelined in favor of so-called *neoclassical economics*, an economic theory widely in use today that, despite its sophistication, treats nature as capital—as a *resource* to be exploited.[12] This, the authors claim, prevents most professional economists from accurately "diagnosing problems, forecasting important trends, and prescribing solutions."

Our inability to share the gifts of nature causes much suffering in the world today. Nature is alive, yet we treat nature as a so-called resource we can own and profit from. For this reason, financial institutions and natural-resource companies are among the most profitable companies in the world. Oil money, for example, fills the coffers of both private corporations and corrupt state officials, while the average person has to struggle to pay for gas. While it's appropriate to compensate companies for their efforts when they convert some of nature's gifts into material goods, why should we allow them to profit from the gifts that nature freely provides to all living beings?

We mistakenly believe that a free market should allow people and corporations to profit from nature, yet we've failed to consider the immense cost to life that occurs whenever people are allowed to reap what they haven't sown at the expense of others. While the privatization of capital can lead to production efficiencies that benefit the entire market, the same can't be said for the privatization of nature: Whenever the income stream from nature is privatized, human beings take for themselves the gifts that would better be freely shared with everyone.

4. SOCIAL DECLINE

"And the great owners, who must lose their land in an up-heaval, the great owners with access to history, with eyes to read history and to know the great fact: when property accumulates in too few hands it is taken away. And that companion fact: when a majority of the people are hungry and cold they will take by force what they need."

—John Steinbeck, *The Grapes of Wrath*

While our current form of capitalism has undoubtedly created an abundance of material wealth, it's also responsible for many of the social problems we have today. We may wonder how the ability to profit from land fosters social dysfunction, but once we realize the extent to which wealth exists in abundance and the extent to which community wealth is privatized for personal gain, we also come to realize just how corrupt most societies actually are. Many social problems exist as a result of how our system *misallocates* wealth, not as a result of an unalterable human condition.

In order to examine the causes of many of our social problems, it's imperative to look at how land values are privatized through our current model of property ownership. Land is prized in our society: Large sums of money change hands in real-estate transactions every day. The value of land changes over time—sometimes it goes up, and sometimes it goes down—although history has shown that as society becomes more prosperous, the value of land tends to rise ahead of inflation.

Communities, not property owners, make land valuable. "But wait," you might say, "if I build a house on a piece of land, I can sell it for more money afterward. The value of a property surely depends on what I do with it." Indeed, the value of a *property* changes: A property with a house on it is more valuable than a similarly sized property nearby that doesn't have a house. However, as long as the wealth of the surrounding community remains unchanged, improvements don't affect the value of the *raw land* upon which they exist in any significant way.[13]

It's important to distinguish the value of raw land from the value of improvements made to land. Whenever we make that essential distinction, we differentiate something that exists by itself in nature—*land*—from something that has been created by human beings: *improvements to land*, such as buildings. To help us better understand that the value of land is *social* in nature, let's imagine a barren plot of land in a desert so far removed from civilization that it can't be of use to any human being. That barren plot of land could be claimed for free since no human being would ever conceive of using it for any purpose; its sales price would therefore be $0. Even if *hundreds of millions* of dollars were poured into the construction of a skyscraper on top of that plot of land, the skyscraper wouldn't be useful to anyone. As long as the building stood alone with no surrounding properties or population—no community benefits or conveniences of any kind—no one would conceive of buying the property for any amount *over the value of its material improvements.* This is why—and this insight is crucial—*land values belong to the communities that have created them*: Land values are socially generated.

The irony is that while improvements such as buildings don't affect the underlying value of the land upon which they are located, they do have the ability to indirectly affect the properties that surround them. They do this by *coalescing* already-existing demand in one location into surrounding land-value increases, much like a cool pane of glass coalesces invisible water vapor into droplets. A hospital building, for example, provides a setting for doctors and nurses to practice in an area, and this increases the quality of life for the people who live in that area, which in turn creates more demand for that particular location. Buildings and other infrastructure, therefore, can indirectly cause land values in the surrounding areas to increase.

Thus far we have discovered three truths about real estate:

1. The value of a property can be divided into the value of its improvements (capital) and the value of the underlying area (land).
2. Improvements made to a property increase the total value of the property, but generally don't change the value of the underlying

land. Instead, land values are socially generated and belong to the communities that
have created them.
3. Buildings can indirectly make surrounding
land more valuable.

If we purchase a property with a house for $250,000
and determine at the time of purchase that the building
itself is worth $100,000, we know that the sales price of
the land itself—the raw land, if no improvements had been
made to it—is worth $150,000. If we sell the property
a year later for $270,000 without making any additional
improvements to it, assuming our building has not deter-
iorated and that there hasn't been any monetary inflation,
our 8 percent profit of $20,000 is entirely due to the
heightened demand for the underlying location. Demand
might have increased because of the presence of an additional population or because of the presence of more
valuable services or infrastructure in the surrounding area.
This profit doesn't arise from any additional value we
may have created for society.

In this example, our 8 percent profit of $20,000 ex-
clusively results from a 13 percent increase in the price
of this particular land in this particular location, now
priced at $170,000 instead of $150,000. The sales price
has simply risen because the community around it became wealthier as a whole. Therefore, when we pocket the
profits from this sale, we're being financially rewarded for

wealth we didn't create; moreover, we receive this reward at the expense of everyone else, since the cost of living and working has become significantly higher for everyone living in the vicinity. Since the value of land is determined by its surroundings, we as a society have for centuries allowed property owners to *privately* reap vast amounts of *socially generated* wealth! This profiting is in actuality an ongoing theft from society, and it leads to greater and greater wealth inequality at the expense of those who don't profit from land.

Since people can only be paid for their goods and services or extract rent from society, less income is available to service the payment of goods and services when proportionally more income is used to pay monopolized rent for land.[14] Essentially, whenever property owners collect rent from rising land values, fewer financial resources are left over for wages and capital investments, and this dynamic can effectively put society on the fast track toward social decline and wealth inequality. As society becomes increasingly wealthy with progressive development, property owners absorb a greater and greater share of society's wealth, leaving less to pay for goods and services.[15] This principle helps explain why wages tend toward a minimum in a materially abundant society: Why do fast-food employees have to hold down two jobs at minimum wage while their employers—the chains themselves, not the franchisees—rake in millions of dollars through their real-estate investment trusts?[16] Why are property developers, who make money by renting out homes in valuable locations, able to command high returns year after year while middle-class homeowners and wage earners have to struggle to pay off their mortgages?

Because we do not differentiate *land* from *capital*, private gains from land-value increases are generally counted as *capital gains*, which is why there's only indirect evidence that correlates wealth inequality to incomes from land.[17] As long as more and more people compete for land in certain locations, and as long as individuals and companies are permitted to reap profits from resulting increases in underlying land values, the forces that perpetuate wealth inequality grow stronger. Given our current system of property ownership, it makes sense that we would see greater *wealth inequality* in places where there's greater *population density* because land values command a greater percentage of the financial resources in the denser areas and only flow into the hands of those who own land.[18] Wages, meanwhile, don't increase proportionally across the board as land becomes more expensive.

As Marcus Aurelius, the great Roman philosopher-king, wrote nearly two thousand years ago, "Poverty is the mother of crime." Whenever a society is increasingly pushed toward greater and greater wealth inequality, everyone is negatively affected. According to one finding published in *The Review of Economics and Statistics*, violent crime in society has a strong correlation to wealth inequality, whereas property crime—not violent crime—

has a strong correlation to poverty and police activity.[19] In other words, while poverty may compel people to steal or damage property, wealth inequality is more likely to compel people to lash out with violence. The psychology behind this pattern isn't difficult to understand: While people may have a tendency to steal out of desperation, they're more likely to commit violence out of anger and frustration if they're faced with high levels of inequality, which evoke a sense of injustice, at least on a subconscious level. These findings are important because they show us that as long as considerable wealth inequality exists—and by implication our ability to profit from land—violent crime is likely to remain a constant part of our human experience.

The ability of individuals to extract wealth from society by profiting from land also leads to *cultural degeneration* and a loss of social cohesion over time. As people converge around a certain location—be it a growing town, city, or metropolis—the demand for land increases. The price of land is bound to increase as a result. In general, as the value of land increases, the return on capital tends to decrease comparatively, which discourages business owners from investing in capital goods and private enterprise. Shrewd investors care about their return on investments, and if land provides a better return on investment than capital, resources will flow away from endeavors that can create jobs, produce wealth, and enliven society, and instead flow into land speculation. As people increasingly extract wealth from society, society will fail to properly harness the regenerative powers of culture and wealth-producing enterprise, and instead incentivize speculative behavior that leads to the corrosion of the social fabric. This cycle eventually *brings about the decline of society itself*.

"There are a thousand hacking at the branches of evil to one who is striking at the root," Henry David Thoreau famously remarked. Conventional approaches that seek to remedy many of our social problems are often only hacking away at the "branches of evil." Every time we address a social issue by making a place more livable, such as through charitable acts or increasing the availability of social services, society's wealth invariably increases; as a result, those who are able to profit from land eventually stand to remove *more* wealth from society at the expense of those who are not. And this is why *even social and technological progress on its own cannot solve the issues* that beset human civilization as long as some can profit from land at the expense of others. Issues such as social decline and crime have to be remedied at their core; if we wish to strike at the root of these issues, we have to share with one another the value of land, and doing so will lead to a better quality of life for everyone. Walt Whitman, one of America's greatest poets, expressed it beautifully:

4. SOCIAL DECLINE

The greatest country, the richest country, is not that which has the most capitalists, monopolists, immense grabbings, vast fortunes, with its sad, sad foil of extreme, degrading, damning poverty, but the land in which there are the most homesteads, freeholds—where wealth does not show such contrasts high and low, where all men have enough—a modest living—and no man is made possessor beyond the sane and beautiful necessities of the simple body and the simple soul.

5. BUSINESS RECESSIONS

The largest asset in every economy is land, followed by buildings, followed by public infrastructure. So what people imagine are industrial economies have remained, basically, land economies.

—Michael Hudson, Professor of Economics,
University of Missouri, Kansas City

Why is something as basic as land still important in our technologically-advanced world? After all, developed nations even have thriving internet economies, where wealth is created virtually yet leads to tangible benefits in the material world. Companies such as Google don't even seem to use significant amounts of land in the vast majority of their business transactions. Or do they?

In order to understand why land is still essential in today's economy, we need to remember that land is the access mechanism by which people and companies benefit from social wealth. Internet conglomerates, for example, benefit from a labor pool of highly skilled employees who live in the neighborhoods that surround their offices; they also benefit from vast technological infrastructures created by countless people and companies over decades, all of which add value to land. These benefits are accessible by *location*, which is in large part why Google was able to become one of the most successful companies in the world: Its success has to be placed in the context of the society in which it exists. Had Google been founded in a developing nation that lacked a highly trained workforce and sophisticated capital infrastructures, its success would have been less likely.

MEDIA 5-1: BILL MOYERS ESSAY: THE UNITED STATES OF INEQUALITY

In California's Silicon Valley Facebook, Google, and Apple are minting millionaires, while the area's homeless are living in tent cities at their virtual doorsteps.

http://unitism.co/theusofinequality

Now let us look at what happens when a society experiences an economic recession or depression. In an economic recession or depression, there seems to be a lower demand for products that were formerly in greater demand, although this isn't really the case: The same human desires that stimulated demand before continue unabated, but now can no longer be satisfied—so technically we still have the same demand as before. What we lack are the same *means* to fulfill that demand. This causes economic activity to constrict, and this constriction can lead to economic recessions and depressions.

In a recession or depression, unemployed workers remain willing to work so that they can afford to buy the things that they continue to desire. And herein lies the crux, the great enigma that economists have wrestled with for centuries: Since there is a continued demand for products and since people have a continued desire to work and produce, why is it that people can't *produce* the goods and services that other people want to buy but can't?

Many economists point to a constriction in the money supply as the root cause of a society's inability to consume. But this conclusion is the economic equivalent of putting the cart before the horse because the creation of wealth must always *precede* the availability of money, since money only functions as a medium in the exchange of wealth. In other words, it isn't a lack of money that fundamentally creates economic contraction, but rather a lack of *wealth production*. For example, when a lone factory in a small town shuts down, the town often experiences an economic depression because the community no longer has the same wealth-producing capacities as before; laid-off factory workers and their families therefore spend less. When demand for goods can't be satisfied because of what seems to be a shortage of money, we're in effect talking about a restriction of wealth production somewhere in the economic cycle, which in turn leads to an eventual reduction in the supply of money (unless it becomes otherwise inflated, such as by central bank decree).

Economists talk a lot about the need for a *consumer economy* (as if consumption alone were the purpose of life, the end-all to happiness and bliss). Yet few economists realize that we can't have a consumer economy if people can't afford to consume, and the only way they can afford to consume over the long run is if they create new wealth to either consume at that time or to defer as investments for later consumption. Simply put, *the best way to have a functioning economy is to focus on having a wealth-producing economy*. But when wealth can't be created in spite of the need for such, the production of wealth has been artificially limited, and this artificial limitation is the root cause of business recessions.

As we recall, there are three factors involved in the production of wealth: nature, human labor, and capital goods. A society undergoing a recession has plenty of un-employed labor to spare, so lack of human labor isn't the constricting factor. And although it's often claimed that the root cause of diminished wealth production is a lack of money (leading to a lack of access to capital goods), lack of money is only the *effect* of a deeper, underlying dysfunction. For example, recent attempts at curing the economic depression in the United States through increases in the money supply have shown that such increases don't necessarily resolve the issues at hand, except to divert more money into the hands of those who already seem to have plenty to spare.

Thus, could it be that the high cost of land restricts the optimal functioning of the economy? Because the cost of land—and therefore the cost of location—directly affects people's abilities to interact and connect with one another in the context of society, the expensive price of land has consequences that reverberate through the *entire* economy and inevitably lead to restriction in the production of wealth throughout society.

In 1983, British economist Fred Harrison published his seminal book *The Power in the Land*, in which he analyzed the economic history of Great Britain since 1701 and noted that property prices—driven by increases in underlying land values—tended to undergo boom-and-bust cycles about every eighteen years.[20] He discovered that these cycles, in turn, affect the business cycle, and not the other way around. In a 2007 article in *MoneyWeek*, Harrison asked the rhetorical question of why many so-called experts haven't been able to accurately predict the direction of the housing market: "Why do these 'experts' get it so wrong? It's because they are working with defective models, which assume that the health of the property market depends upon the condition of the rest of the economy. In fact, my research suggests that property is the key factor that shapes the business cycle, not the other way around."[21]

Harrison explains in *The Power in the Land* how land values over time become so expensive that too little wealth is left to pay for goods and services. The reason land becomes too expensive too quickly is because real-estate speculation allows property owners to demand prices for land that are higher than the economy can realistically sustain. In a sense, property owners have the ability to demand *tomorrow's* wealth output *today*, because they have the power to withhold land from use and public enjoyment in expectation of future gains. This process creates an artificial constriction in the supply of land, which makes the price of land increase at a rate the economy cannot sustain. But because people can't compromise on basic subsistence, land eventually becomes unaffordable, and the price of land contracts simply because it has to. At the same time, businesses are no longer able to make a profit after paying for rent and mortgages: Production stalls while consumption drops; a depression ensues. In time, once wages have sufficiently recovered, a new cycle begins, and the whole process starts all over again: Land values eventually increase until they reach a point where they grow so much that they then forcibly contract once more, leading to another depression, and so forth.

These major business cycles happen on average about every eighteen years, and are usually punctuated by a single, brief recession along the way. According to Harrison, the property cycle generally undergoes a fourteen-year upswing: The first seven years are a recovery phase from the previous bust, after which a seven-year boom phase ensues. This boom phase includes a two-year run-up in real-estate prices toward the end, and it's inevitably followed by a severe price correction that lasts about three to five years.[22] Harrison's observations were so on point that he went on record to accurately predict not only the timing of the major depression of 1992, but also the global

2008–2010 depression in 1997—*eleven years before the depression occurred:*[23]

> The property boom of 2000 will come as a shock to Gordon Brown [who was Britain's Chancellor of the Exchequer at the time, and later, in 2007, became Britain's Prime Minister], who, if he is still presiding in Britain's Treasury in the first decade of the millennium, will . . . be politically traumatised by the astronomical unearned gains from land that will be pocketed by shrewd operators who know how to manipulate the tax system. . . . The consequence is predictable. By 2007 Britain and most of the other industrially advanced economies will be in the throes of frenzied activity in the land market equal to what happened in 1988/9. Land prices will be near their 18-year peak, driven by an exponential growth rate, on the verge of collapse that will presage the global depression of 2010. The two events will not be coincidental: the peak in land prices not merely signaling the looming recession but being the primary cause of it.

Fred E. Foldvary is another prominent economist who *also* published his timely predictions of the 2008–2010 depression in 1997: "The 18-year cycle in the U.S. and similar cycles in other countries gives [this] cycle theory predictive power: the next major bust, 18 years after the 1990 downturn, will be around 2008, if there is no major interruption such as a global war."[24] He goes on to explain in greater detail how land speculation causes economic depressions:

> When a boom is underway, the anticipated increase in rent induces speculators to buy land for price appreciation rather than for present use, which causes the current site value to rise above that warranted by present use. Once widespread speculation sets in, land values are carried beyond the point at which enterprises can make a profit after paying for rent or mortgages. The rate of increase of investment slows down, eventually reducing aggregate demand as the slowdown ripples through the economy, increasing unemployment and bringing forth a depression. Thus a fall in demand follows the initial cause, the rising cost of land.

One of the key characteristics of science is predictability: If we can't make accurate predictions, the model we're using is faulty. If, on the other hand, we can have a general idea of outcomes based on a predictable pattern, then our economic model warrants a closer look. Like a prophet drawing from both his scientific experience and his intuitive insight, Foldvary issued another warning in an article he published in March 2012 titled *"The Depression of 2026"*:[25]

> If shocks [from outside the U.S. economy] don't interrupt the cycle, the deep fiscal and monetary

structures of the U.S. economy, which have not changed in 200 years, will generate the next boom and bust just as they have done so in the past. But the Crash of 2026 will be much worse than that of 2008, because as the U.S. government continues its annual trillion-dollar deficits, by 2024 the U.S. debt will have grown so large that U.S. bonds will no longer be considered safe, and in the financial crisis the U.S. will no longer be able to borrow the funds needed to bail out the financial firms. Americans still have time to prevent the next great boom and bust, but they are culturally bound to the status quo, as are almost all economists, so the warnings will go unheeded as they did during the 1990s and 2000s. We are now far upstream, but heading down into the river of no return to the real estate and financial waterfall of 2024–2026.

Will it happen? Strong tendencies seem to move us in this direction. Unfortunately, many politicians today—and homeowners bound to expensive mortgages—want properties to become more expensive in order to help the economy out of its recession. What most people don't yet realize is that *the value of land is best shared*, and that whenever we profit from land, we profit from society. Indigenous peoples have long known this ancient and timeless wisdom, of course, yet we've forgotten it. Chief Crowfoot of the Siksika First Nation in southern Alberta, Canada, for example, reminds us, "As long as the sun shines and the waters flow, this land will be here to give life to men and animals. We cannot sell the lives of men and animals. The land was put here by the Great Spirit and we cannot sell it because it does not belong to us."[26] We in the modern age have forgotten this simple truth; our entire economy is built upon this one presumption that nature is property. The next business cycle will unravel before we know it, and it won't be too long before we'll have to deal with the next major depression and the immense personal impact that our ongoing profiting from land will have upon our lives.

6. ECOCIDE

Our global economic system is a subsystem of a larger system: the larger system is the biosphere and the subsystem is the economy. The problem, of course, is that our subsystem, the economy, is geared for growth whereas the parent system remains the same size. So as the economy grows, it encroaches upon the biosphere, and this is the fundamental opportunity cost of economic growth.

—Herman E. Daly, former Senior Economist at
the World Bank

Many of us have driven through the countryside and beheld the beauty of rolling hills and valleys, open prairies and rugged deserts, as well as admired the dazzling variety and intricacies of flora, fauna, and terrain. But unless we're driving through a public park or nature preserve, most of the land we see is likely surrounded by barbed wire and "No Trespassing" signs. We've come to understand that all land not explicitly designated for public use is privately owned by individual people or groups, regardless of whether it's put to use or not. *Millions upon millions* of privately owned acres contribute to an artificially created scarcity in a world of plenty. We collectively occupy far more land than we actually *need,* in anticipation of the future gains we might be able to extract as a result of the scarcity we ourselves have created.

The next time you pass by a property that's only minimally used but nonetheless owned, consider how harmless it seems. You might even think that the private ownership may have preserved a little piece of nature from human contact; otherwise, perhaps human beings would have frivolously inhabited it, just as we seem to inhabit any and all other lands that we find freely available.

However, this perspective only arises because of the scarcity we have collectively created; such a situation would not occur if we only used as much land as we actually needed. If our *exclusive* use of land came with an ongoing responsibility to our local community, nature would no longer be exploited: Most people would tend to use no more land than absolutely necessary. Acreage would be used far more efficiently, and the cost of land would simultaneously become far more affordable to those who make efficient use of it. Consider this thought the next time you see land marked "No Trespassing."

The destruction of nature is the direct result of a severely dysfunctional economic system, a system we have created ourselves over millennia. Without any doubt, we as a species are committing ongoing *ecocide*: the destruction of our own habitat. Nature can be—and, of course, already has been—altered to such an extent that various life-forms can no longer support themselves in certain areas. We're already paying a steep price for the destruction of nature, measured not only in dollars but in the suffering of billions of human beings and other life-forms all over the world. This destruction has increasingly irreparable consequences; meanwhile, the root issues are not properly understood and are left unchecked.[27]

So far, we've learned that our hoarding of land creates a localized sense of scarcity. Because of this artificially created scarcity, human beings all over the Earth seek to supplement their meager incomes through the additional exploitation of nature—usually not for productive but for *speculative* purposes. It doesn't take too much imagination to realize that as long as people and institutions are allowed to profit from land at the expense of other people, we're enabling a system that *incentivizes* the destruction of our own habitat. This happens in three primary ways.

First, since human beings are allowed to profit not only from their goods and services but also from nature, we encourage the pillaging of nature to supplement incomes. Our incomes, however, are already relatively meager due to the unequal sharing of natural and social wealth. By allowing people to profit from land, we give them an incentive to harm their own communities through the reckless destruction of our planet's delicate ecology.

Second, because our ability to profit from land at the expense of our communities is firmly entrenched in our economic system, and because, as a result, existing land is priced far above its actual value while wages and capital returns are taxed, the cost of living is significantly higher for all members of society than it really should be. This high cost of living requires human beings to extend themselves and their economic activities far beyond levels actually necessary to support their ongoing existence. And since most economic activity heavily depends upon our extensive use of raw materials and generates enormous amounts of nonbiodegradable waste, any additional wasteful economic activity by default comes with a steep ecological price tag.

And third, our current model of land ownership encourages a sprawl of human civilization as populations seek out land that's still available at a lesser cost. For example, land that's held speculatively and not put to productive use inside a city or a town is a major reason people live in suburban communities far from their places of employment, resulting in the kind of urban sprawl and suburban dystopia often seen throughout North America. This very mechanism is also responsible for the destruction of rainforests. In the areas where rainforest destruction is epidemic, wealth inequality and land ownership rates are particularly disproportionate; millions of acres of prime farmland are owned by only a few and are used mostly for grazing instead of farming purposes. This status quo naturally forces many to slash and burn large areas of the rainforest in their quest to obtain land just so that they can simply make a living for themselves.[28]

In 2007, a team of researchers from McGill University of Montréal, Québec, Canada, published a study that correlated heightened levels of wealth inequality to increased biodiversity loss. The results were so astounding that the study was repeated in 2009, but with more complex models, to similar results. The researchers discovered that a nation's *economic footprint* provides a close enough correlation to be statistically significant, particularly if taken together with its level of income inequality. A nation's economic footprint is the size of its economy relative to its geographical size, that is, relative to the size of its land mass. The fact that a nation's economic footprint provides significant correlation to biodiversity loss should come as no surprise; if a nation's economy is large compared with its amount of land, land will increasingly be hoarded, and this hoarding will invariably have a significant impact upon the ecology. This dynamic is particularly interesting if we consider that the income inequality factor provides us with an additional correlation, and income inequality, as we know, can be traced back to the hoarding of land.

In their biodiversity study, the researchers mentioned another study that highlighted the unequal sharing of nature as a potential cause of both wealth inequality and loss of biodiversity: "A study of community forestry in Mexico showed that village forest management was correlated with levels of inequality. In a village with an economic structure that was highly unequal, forests were managed poorly because small groups of powerful people manipulated the logging industry for their own benefit, resulting in overexploitation. In more equitable villages, however, community institutions were more effective, resulting in better forest management and likely less biodiversity loss." Could it be that whenever nature is hoarded we'll see greater wealth inequality and biodiversity loss? Common sense on its own points to a correlation between our profiting from nature and the loss of biodiversity.

We're indeed living within a system that encourages us as a species to behave like a tumor that relentlessly attacks its host in a futile effort to prolong its own existence; we're devouring ourselves and nature in the process. Will our collective conscience wake up to the realities of such a system—a system that encourages us to wastefully consume and destroy nature for ultimately no good reason? As the author Barbara Kingsolver has remarked, "The feeling that morality has nothing to do with the way we use the resources of the world is an idea that can't persist much longer. If it does, then we won't."

7. EARTH, OUR HOME

*We abuse land because we regard it as a commodity belonging
to us. When we see land as a community to which we belong,
we may begin to use it with love and respect.*

Aldo Leopold (1887–1948)

The Earth sustains all life. Whether we believe life orig-
inated through evolution, intelligent design, or divine
creation doesn't change the reality that the Earth continues to sustain us today. It's a fact that anyone, regardless
of nationality, worldview, or religion, can agree on. But
humanity is a fractured species at heart; we've separated
ourselves from nature, and then further subdivided one
another by gender, nationality, race, religion, ethnicity,
sexual orientation, social status, economic class, and so
forth. In doing so, we too often forget that every human being is an integral part of this beautiful blue mar-
ble floating through time and space. We believe that the
Earth belongs to us, but we seem to forget that, in truth,
we belong to the Earth. At its root, our economic crisis is
a crises in consciousness because we see ourselves as separate from our *environment*, when, in reality, we're inextri-
cably connected to all that is.[29] As a result, we've deluded
ourselves into thinking that land should be owned and
then profited from by some at the expense of others.

The preceding chapters have given us glimpses of what happens—and how—when we fail to share the surplus of nature and society with one another. And while we as human beings disagree on almost everything under the stars, the recognition that this Earth—and all the land upon it—is our common home ought to be foundation upon which all our perspectives and philosophies come to rest. We need to make this recognition the starting and ending point of any discussion of an economic model that's both efficient and just. Anything other than unconditional acceptance and an implementation of this truth is but a compromise and a muddling of an otherwise clear and universal principle: No single human being has an intrinsic right to profit from that which, ultimately, cannot belong to anyone at all.

Land has been privatized nearly *everywhere*; this privatization is endemic to the entire system. We don't consider the impact that our individual actions have upon the totality of life as we seek to grab as big a share of land as we can. Maybe a part of us knows, deep down, that our destructive economic system doesn't provide abundantly for those of us who don't profit from land in some shape or another, or maybe our desires just seem to keep growing in lockstep with our appropriation of material wealth. Either way, at the root of our motivation to take and own lies a gnawing fear—a fear of losing out and of not having enough.

The scriptures of all major religions advise against hoarding land for these very reasons. The Judeo-Christian tradition, for example, is unmistakably clear that nature is a *gift* (Genesis 9:1–3, among other passages). It even prohibits permanent land ownership and provides land-leasing guidance (Leviticus 25), while expressly stating that "the profit of the land is for all" (Ecclesiastes 5:9).[30] Ancient Hindu sages stated that "the soil is the common property of all" and that people shall "through their own efforts, enjoy the fruits thereof."[31] In Islam, the prophet Muhammad expressed it quite succinctly when he stated that "the people are partners in three things: water, pastures, and fire" (Sultaniyya Hadith 26), which could be interpreted as "water, land, and energy." And while the Buddha didn't explicitly address the land issue, he taught that the practice of *right livelihood* was essential on the path of enlightenment. Since it's almost universally understood in Buddhism that stealing is contrary to the spirit of right livelihood, we have to assume that the profiting from land is therefore also contrary to the Buddhist spiritual path. A similar principle exists for practitioners of the yogic traditions: The third yama of Patanjali's Yoga Sutras is *asteya*, or nonstealing. And most indigenous cultures on Earth treat nature as gift, not property; although many Native American tribes and First Nations people have sporadically fought one another over certain territory, the battles were about the right of use of land—never ownership, which is a concept foreign to most indigenous cultures.[32]

It's time to recognize that all beings have a sustainable right of access to nature's abundance. It's a fundamental birthright. Indeed, the equal and sustainable right of access to the Earth's bounty seems one of the most transcendent truths a human being can ever contemplate. But this fundamental right is missing from the *United Nations Universal Declaration of Human Rights*, despite the declaration's first article stating, "All human beings are born free and equal in dignity and rights." The fact that this single principle is violated on an ongoing basis is quite possibly the root cause of many, if not most, other human rights violations.[33]

Even though a five-year-old might recognize the importance of sharing nature's abundance, many economists today continue to deny that nature has to be shared. Some economists mistakenly attempt to apply supposedly free market principles to the privatization of nature. For example, libertarian economist Murray Rothbard made several basic thought mistakes when he wrote:

> Well, what about idle land? Should the sight of it alarm us? On the contrary, we should thank our stars for one of the greatest facts of nature: that labor is scarce relative to land. It is a fact that there is more land available in the world, even quite useful land, than there is labor to keep it employed. This is a cause for rejoicing, not lament.

A simple analysis of the above paragraph reveals that even a distinguished economist such as Rothbard can make thought mistakes of fundamental proportions. In this case, he fails to distinguish land in *undesired* locations from land in *desired* locations. If land indeed is freely available as he claims it is, why then does it have a cost that varies from location to location? Labor isn't scarce relative to land in desirable locations—far from it: *Land* is exceptionally scarce in desirable locations, which is why land in a city costs a lot more than land in the countryside. Land in most locations isn't freely available; otherwise, it could be had for free. Instead, it's owned—regardless of whether it's used or not—and thus made scarce.[34]

Sometimes, common sense can be missing when we look at a subject and fail to recognize problems that are self-evident. If advanced education lacks common sense, it doesn't make us immune to thought mistakes at a foundational level; some trained economists don't seem to think that the gifts of nature ought to be equitably shared for the benefit of all. Career pressures might also play a role: Upton Sinclair, one of America's most prolific writers, famously said, "It is difficult to convince a man of something when his salary depends on his not understanding it." Yet considering the influence that many economists have in today's public discourse, they can't afford to uphold the failed economic policies of old much longer. As stewards of the knowledge that has the power to free humanity from the shackles of poverty and self-destruction, their duty is to rise above partisanship and devote themselves to the well-being of the general public and, therefore, to the preservation of our shared natural, cultural, and economic legacy.

PART II: A NEW PARADIGM
FOR A THRIVING WORLD

A new consciousness is developing
which sees the Earth as a single organism
and recognizes that an organism at war with itself is doomed.
We are one planet.
One of the great revelations of the age of space exploration
is the image of the Earth finite and lonely,
somehow vulnerable,
bearing the entire human species
through the oceans of space and time.

—Carl Sagan (1934–1996)

8. RESTORING COMMUNITIES

A proper community is a commonwealth: a place, a resource, an economy. It answers the needs, practical as well as social and spiritual, of its members—among them the need to need one another. The answer to the present alignment of political power with wealth is the restoration of the identity of community and economy.

—Wendell Berry

Every being on this planet is imbued with consciousness simply by virtue of their existence. Each being has an innate nobility, a dignity that can't be tarnished, though the suffering of our human experience often blinds us to this reality. We're all intimately connected to all that is, because we're a part of life. When we seek to own a part of nature, we usually do so because we see ourselves as separate from nature. Yet we are deeply interconnected to one another and the Earth. And since every human being *needs* land in order to simply exist, doesn't it follow that the value that land freely offers to all human beings would best be freely shared with all?

Aside from the ethical implications that arise when we don't share the value of land with one another, we'll continue to experience a host of challenging issues as long as the value of land remains privatized. Do we wish

to solve poverty, reverse the process of cultural degeneration, and halt the cancerous destruction of nature? Then
we're wise to begin to share the gifts of nature with one
another.

While it's infeasible in practical terms for us to share
every aspect of nature with one another, it's entirely possible for us to share the *monetary value* that human beings
assign to nature. Once we begin to share this value with
one another, we have the opportunity to unleash a cultural, technological, ecological, and even spiritual renais-
sance that will liberate us in ways we can't even begin
to imagine! Once we truly begin to share these financial
resources, we *can* create a world where everyone can have
their basic needs met, where nature is no longer exploited,
where people are given the greatest opportunities for self-
expression, and where life is not just an array of setbacks,
but a beautiful canvas that allows for a greater unfolding
of human potential.

If we're to share the value of land, it's certainly not necessary to abolish the exclusive *use* of land. On the contrary, the forcible seizing of land from individuals by
government without just compensation deserves to be
called tyranny. The fundamental thing we need to abolish is the *mechanism* by which people unfairly profit from
land.[35] The solution is so simple that it's most often over-
looked: *Property owners merely need to pay the communities from
which they receive benefits through their exclusive use of land the
exact market value of the benefits that they receive.*

Property owners—and all those with a vested interest in properties, including, and perhaps even *especially*, financial institutions—benefit enormously from the communities in which their properties are located. Profits from land are not only unearned but also deplete community resources, which need to be replenished periodically. This replenishment can best be accomplished through a *land leasehold model* in which land is owned in common, even as it is privately used, since the rental value of land reflects the combined value of all the natural and social benefits that people receive through their possession and exclusive use of land. When land users pay significant portions of the rental value of land to their local communities, they rightfully reimburse their communities. When land users make such contributions to their local communities, they make what I call *community land contributions*.

Community land contributions are similar to so-called *land-value taxes*, a method by which property owners are taxed on the value of the land they possess. Unlike community land contributions, however, land-value taxes are still rooted in the paradigm of private land ownership: They use the selling price of land as a tax base to determine the tax obligation of the landowner; to reference the selling price of land instead of its rental value psychologically already implies private land ownership as opposed to community land stewardship that allows for private land use. The word *tax* also implies that the people being taxed have to part with something that belongs to them, since people pay taxes on *their* incomes, *their* sales, *their* capital gains, and so forth. The term *land-value tax*, therefore, implies that land users are being taxed on *their* land value, which, of course, is incorrect, because the *value* of land belongs to the communities that create that value. *Community land contributions*, on the other hand, appropriately emphasize that land is a community good and that people ought to contribute to their communities if they choose to use it exclusively.

A community land contribution model would allow us to move from a *monopoly model* on land toward a competitive *leasing model* in such a way that people can continue to use land exclusively if they so wish, except that now other people are reimbursed for their exclusion. When community land contributions are made at frequent intervals (for example, annually) and as a fraction of the market rental value of land (for example, 80 percent of rental value), land users begin to pay their communities for their use of land instead of other human beings or institutions (such as the seller from whom the land was bought or the bank that provides the mortgage). Such ongoing payments to our local communities have the effect of lowering the selling price of land in relation to the rental value of land: They tend to approximate the market rental value of land and will never be greater than what land users would pay had they otherwise leased the land on the open market.[36]

Historically, there have been periods when people shared the value of land with their local communities due to the economic policies of the time. Too often, however, these economic policies didn't go far enough, and the resulting wealth wasn't always shared in ways that remedied poverty and decreased wealth inequality. One of the more modern examples is Hong Kong, a former British Crown colony in Southeast Asia. Since the end of the Second World War, Hong Kong has experienced an economic boom on a meteoric scale; within just a few decades, this small, relatively unknown city became one of the world's dominant centers of high finance. Since all land was considered to belong to the British Crown,[37] the British colonial government leased land to private entities.[38] These leaseholds have allowed Hong Kong to collect a certain amount of land value and have also allowed the government to maintain relatively low tax rates.[39]

Although it's often cited as a model of laissez-faire economic growth due to its low income and corporate tax rates, its minimal interference in economic affairs, and its lack of sovereign debt, Hong Kong practiced, in effect, a form of conventional capitalism while simply preventing—at least to a small extent—its residents from profiting too much from land. Yet even though Hong Kong's leasehold model represents a step in the right direction, it remains flawed since land-value assessments are not updated annually to reflect the current market value of land; leasehold revenues therefore bear little relationship to yearly increases in land values. On the other hand, because Hong Kong is a relatively small island of prosperity, it has also had to deal with massive immigration from mainland China, and because Hong Kong's land values were not widely shared with all Hong Kong residents, this influx created massive poverty problems in Hong Kong as well.[40] We can only imagine what kind of prosperity Hong Kong might achieve for all its residents if it were to fully share the value of its land.

In other examples, today every resident of Alaska receives a relatively modest Basic Income from the value of oil.[41] Norway does something similar, though on a much bigger scale, with its *Government Pension Fund—Global*, a fund entirely financed through revenues from Norway's petroleum sector and currently the largest pension fund in the world.[42] The island of Taiwan was able to achieve rapid economic success without causing severe wealth inequality once it implemented land-reform policies.[43] Central California's transformation from dust bowl to breadbasket of America in the late 1800s is another example of natural wealth shared for public benefit: The State of California constructed vast irrigation infrastructures financed entirely through the taxation of resulting land-value increases.[44] Whenever society chooses to safeguard nature for the benefit of current and future generations, the wealth that becomes available to society is *immense*: Every time the value of land is shared, the economy balances, nature is conserved, land speculation is inhibited, and society becomes more prosperous overall.

So how can we implement economic policies that share the value of land? The problem is that in most nations around the world the value of land is already privatized: If communities were to suddenly impose land contributions upon existing property owners, property owners would end up having to pay *twice* for their use of land—first to the previous owner (from whom they bought land) and then again to their local communities.[45] It is a challenging ethical dilemma: On the one hand, no one should be asked to pay twice for something they only agreed to pay for once. On the other hand, it's appropriate for property owners to reimburse their local communities for their exclusive use of land—if they don't, everyone ends up being worse off in the end.

Of course, governments could financially compensate existing property owners with government bonds: Fred E. Foldvary—the aforementioned economist who correctly timed the 2008 recession in 1997—recommends this approach.[46] To implement a compensation plan would require a large-scale societal transformation, however: All levels of government and society would have to work together to accomplish such a monumental undertaking.[47] While it's certainly possible, such a transformation is unlikely given society's current lack of awareness regarding the underlying economic realities that drive our choices and behaviors. What other options might we have at our disposal in order to create social change? We demonstrate a deep understanding of the process of social change when we realize that it isn't an idea alone that matters, but the *practice* of it, no matter how small the implementation of our idea may be at first. In other words, we are called to implement new models of land stewardship that render our existing model of land ownership obsolete.

One such new model was conceived by the late Adrian Wrigley, a Cambridge academic who envisioned a model based on *land-use rights*.[48] What's interesting about his model is that land-use rights enable communities to collect the value of land while also permitting private land use at the same time. In essence, land-use rights are voluntarily created between a community and a property owner: When real estate is put up for sale, either the local government or a community land trust advances funds to the new buyer to pay for the land-value portion of the sales price.[49] In exchange for these funds, the buyer receives a tradable land-use right for the property.[50] According to Wrigley: "The owner of the property is required to pay an index-linked sum to the community [for his land-use right] on a monthly basis in perpetuity. The land-value mortgage paperwork is handled by a bank, and when completed, the government pays the bank and the bank lodges the [land-use right] in return. The bank has no further involvement with the arrangement." A property tied to a land-use right should be exempt from property taxes, and community land contributions made by the title holder should ideally be tax-deductible on state and federal levels as well.

Unlike taxes, which are enforced by governments upon property owners and tenants alike, land-use rights involve a voluntary arrangement between an individual and the local community to which the individual belongs. This creates a mutually beneficial bond for everyone involved: The community recognizes the voluntary nature of the transaction and tends to appreciate the willingness of the land user to reimburse the community for the exclusive use of land. And since land users will have to financially invest in their local communities on an ongoing basis through community land contributions, they're more likely to become interested in maintaining the well-being of their communities. The land user, meanwhile, will no doubt appreciate the ability to use land without having to pay a substantial amount upfront.

We'll look at land-use rights in greater detail in later chapters. But before we do that, let's take a closer look at our current tax system, because taxes, as we shall see, profoundly influence the way we interact with one another. Currently, people pay very little for the benefits they receive through their possession of land to the communities that provide these benefits. And so, to pay for public works, governments are forced to tax the production and consumption activities of their citizens instead.

Since tax systems create behavioral incentives for *billions* of people worldwide, and since our economies by and large currently tend to incentivize the unequal sharing of land, we can effectively remedy a whole plethora of economic, social, and ecological issues by sharing the value of land. Once we do, we can effectively change *how billions of people behave economically, socially, and ecologically.* If this conclusion is indeed true, we can potentially make the greatest difference for our planet and for humanity by focusing our efforts on eliminating tax systems and encouraging people to share nature's gifts instead.

9. KEEP WHAT YOU EARN,
PAY FOR WHAT YOU USE

It is better to pay a small amount of rent on your block of land than to pay a large amount in income tax and indirect taxation.

—Australian politician Clyde Cameron (1913–2008)

Few people enjoy reading about taxes, and it's probably true that even fewer people enjoy paying them. Many of us have good reasons for not wanting to pay taxes: More often than not, taxes take significant portions of the wealth that we've created through our own efforts. For many of us, taxes limit our ability to make our best contributions to society; they often seem to stifle our material and intellectual aspirations. Tax systems are essentially the mechanisms by which societies decide *what people have to share with each other versus what they can keep for themselves*, and societies enforce these mechanisms on *billions* of people every day. Since tax systems play such an important role in life, let's look more closely at taxes and see what alternatives exist.

As we'll discover in this chapter, societies that share in the gifts of nature don't need to raise taxes. Contemporary societies are forced to tax people's contributions to their local communities because the ownership of land makes people extract resources from society on an ongoing basis—social resources that need to be periodically replenished. If instead we shared the value of land with one another, we would no longer require taxes to replenish those social resources.

Let's look at several traits that all public revenue systems need to embody in order to work harmoniously. In "The Ultimate Tax Reform: Public Revenue from Land Rents," Foldvary recommends five such essential traits. According to Foldvary, sources of public revenue have to be:

1. Efficient
2. Simple
3. Transparent
4. Fair
5. Revenue sufficient

In this light, let's examine whether land contributions have the potential to replace conventional taxes and see if they can meet all five requirements.

MEDIA 9-1: THE ULTIMATE TAX REFORM: PUBLIC REVENUE FROM LAND RENT

In this paper, economist Fred Foldvary takes a closer look at land contributions and their implications for society.

http://unitism.co/ultimatereform

In order to be *efficient* (the first of our criteria), public revenue collection would affect production and consumption only minimally, if at all.[51] The terms *deadweight loss* and *excess burden* are used in economics to describe the negative effects that taxes create on production and consumption activities: Because production and consumption taxes (such as income, payroll, and sales taxes) increase the prices of goods and services, we have to produce more goods and services overall, yet are enjoying fewer of them. These taxes drain resources from where they're most needed, but don't use them as efficiently elsewhere.

The payroll tax, for example, punishes businesses and entrepreneurs for creating jobs for the economy, while consumption taxes such as sales taxes discourage access to perhaps much-needed goods; capital gains taxes deter investments, while property taxes on buildings discourage the creation of affordable housing and inhibit the beautification of neighborhoods. In short, our current tax system is in most respects a lose-lose proposition.

But what would happen if we shared land instead? Community land contributions are payments for the use of land. A system based on land contributions wouldn't harm production or consumption because people would continue to use land to produce and consume, except that now they would use only as much land as they actually needed. Since land contributions encourage people to use land efficiently, they don't decrease the profitability of productive enterprise as long as land is used well; land contributions don't cause any deadweight loss and are therefore highly efficient.

Let's pause for a moment to imagine a world in which you and I didn't have to pay taxes and instead simply paid a community contribution for our use of land:

- If you're an *employee*, imagine what it might be like if your final take-home salary were exactly the gross amount that's written on your paycheck, not the net amount. Your personal income would increase substantially without the payment of an income tax. And with land no longer hoarded, involuntary unemployment could mostly become a thing of the past.

- As a *consumer*, imagine a world in which you no longer had to pay any sales or value-added taxes. You could buy more for less.

- If you're a *business owner*, picture what life might be like if your business didn't have to pay the payroll tax. Employees would cost less, and you might even be able to hire more employees and increase your profitability at the same time.

- If you're a *shareholder*, think of how your bottom line would increase with the removal of the corporate income tax.

- If you're an *investor* and own stocks, mutual funds, or a retirement fund, consider the benefits of not having to pay taxes on your capital gains. And because the companies you own also wouldn't have to pay payroll, sales, capital gains, and corporate income taxes, the value of your portfolio is likely to grow significantly.

- If you're a *homeowner*, imagine no longer having to pay a property tax. You would still pay for the land you use, but that amount would never be greater than what the land is actually worth to you. In other words, it would be as if you own your house but lease the land at a discounted market rate. The savings you'd incur from the removal of all other taxes would more than likely offset the periodic land contributions that would be applied to your property's location value. But what if the location value of your home increases and you can no longer afford to make a land contribution to your local community as a result of that increase? A location value increase means that your community has more to offer, and you, as a member of your local community, stand to benefit. In the unlikely event that you don't benefit from the increased wealth present in your local community and are unable to make sufficient land contributions to your local community, you can accumulate liens on the land until you transfer the property or die, as is commonly done today with real-estate taxes. The best way to prevent this from happening would be for your community to offer you a Universal Basic Income. We'll talk more about the Universal Basic Income in Chapter 11, Affordable Housing.

- If you're a *prospective homebuyer*, you would likely have more money to buy a property (as a result of the aforementioned points), and the property would likely be more affordable.

- If you're a *retired homeowner* without any income except social security, you would still be better off than the countless other retirees who have to rent land *and* homes during their retirement years. Furthermore, food and other goods would cost less because they wouldn't be burdened by taxes. And if communities instituted a Universal Basic Income, retirees wouldn't have to worry at all.

- If you're a *farmer*, you'd pay a land contribution for the land in your care. Your farmland contribution would never be greater than the land's unimproved rental value, and if used both efficiently and productively, the land would always yield a surplus. As the steward of this land, you would retain all the existing rights to use the land in whatever ways permissible by law.

- The only people who would end up paying more money are those who use land inefficiently or those who seek to profit from it directly. Banks, real estate developers, mining industries, and other extractive industries that generally take more than their fair share would instead be forced to accept more reasonable profit margins.

Do these points sound too good to be true? Of course they do. We're so accustomed to our current reality that this potential reality sounds too unrealistic—but it only sounds that way because it doesn't exist right now, not because it can't be achieved. "It always seems impossible until it's done," Nelson Mandela once remarked. Right now, our economies are hugely inefficient and we're destroying nature in the process, so the possibility of material abundance for everyone in a sustainable system sounds like a pipe dream. If, however, we stop treading water and allow constructive activities to occur in the proper context, our society can naturally experience this kind of abundance.

The excess burden that arises from our misallocation of resources created through our current tax system lies at the heart of many contemporary political debates; whenever people advocate for small government or a reformation of the tax system, the intent is usually to see a decrease in the economy's deadweight loss in order to make the overall economy more *efficient*. The thinking goes that if government spends less, it won't have to raise as much money through taxation, which, conventional experience tells us, tends to hold the economy back. And although a decrease in the economy's deadweight loss can be achieved through a reduction in various taxes, it can be done far more effectively, at far higher gain and at much lower cost, through a simple shift away from taxes toward a system that allows us to share in the gifts of nature.

Foldvary recommends that land contributions make up about 80 percent of a land's rental value; it's generally good to leave some benefit to homeowners and other land users since this practice allows room for assessment errors and also allows the real-estate market to function more optimally. If a plot of land could be leased out for about $6,000 per year, the property would cost the land user about $4,800 per year to use ($4,800 is 80 percent of $6,000). The good news is that because this piece of land now has a cost of $4,800 per year, its sales price falls in relation to its leasing price. While the land might previously have sold for $150,000, it might now sell for only $40,000 (more information on how community land contributions influence property values will be provided in the Appendix). These land contributions apply only to land. Property taxes are *not* comparable to land contributions because a land contribution doesn't apply to the total value of the property if the property has improvements such as buildings; it just applies to the value of the underlying *land*, which in this way is shared.[52]

Our second criterion is simplicity. Public revenue systems need to be *simple* if they're to be beneficial. How can we expect people to live abundant lives when much of their time is spent preparing tax returns that eat into the time they may have set aside for work, family, and leisure activities? U.S. tax returns, for example, are anything but simple: The Taxpayer Advocate Service, a branch of the U.S. Internal Revenue Service (IRS), estimates in its 2010 Annual Report to Congress that U.S. taxpayers and businesses spend about *6.1 billion hours filing their taxes each year*. If all of these hours were outsourced, it could provide *year-round, full-time employment to about three million workers*.[53] In addition, the cost of tax compliance in the U.S. is estimated at $163 billion, which is 11 percent of total income tax receipts.[54] If tax compliance were an industry, *it would be one of the largest industries in the United States*.[55] The IRS tax code itself has grown so long that its length can't even be determined uniformly. In its 2010 Annual Report, the Taxpayer Advocate Service estimates that the tax code contains about 3.8 million words; if printed on U.S. letter-sized paper, it would require about 15,200 pages. Complexity in a tax system unnecessarily wastes wealth without providing any offsetting benefits to either the taxpayer or the government. Once more we realize that our present tax system falls woefully short: It is not only inefficient but also needlessly complex.

But what about community land contributions? Land contributions are relatively simple for the obvious reason that they're somewhat fixed in value; they're based on the market rental value of land, which ought to be assessed at least once a year. They also have no deductibles and little bureaucracy attached. In his work "The Ultimate Tax Reform," Foldvary writes that with land contributions "there would no longer be any tax audits. There would be no record-keeping for taxes. You would instead get a monthly bill, like you get for utilities. You would simply pay the bill or have it automatically deducted from some financial account. At the same time, government would avoid the high cost of processing complex accounts and keeping individual tax records. It would only need to keep real estate records and assess the land values, both of which it already does for property tax purposes."

Although critics sometimes claim that an accurate assessment of land values is difficult, there are several effective standard methods. Professional real-estate appraisers routinely separate land values from building values for fire-insurance purposes, among other reasons. In contrast to property tax assessments, where the assessor needs to enter the property to inspect the various buildings and determine their value, land-value assessments are nonintrusive since generally no on-the-ground inspection is necessary. Figures garnered from property sales—together with vacant-land sales data and commercial real-estate leasing figures—can be put into computerized models through which assessors can determine land values for each general location; contrary to property values, which are heavily influenced by the value of individual buildings, land values usually vary only slightly from one neighboring plot to another. Foldvary recommends that the computerized mapping service be implemented in such a way as to "emphasize long-term trends rather than year-by-year fluctuations in land values."

MEDIA 9-2: A COMPUTERIZED MODEL OF LAND VALUES

In this video, Gabriel Ahlfeldt, lecturer at the London School of Economics, presents a unique spatiotemporal dataset of Chicago's historical land values, providing insights into changes in the spatial structure of the city.

http://unitism.co/landvalueassessment

Any effective public revenue system also needs to be *transparent*—our third criterion—in order to make it innately safe from abuse, corruption, and unwarranted government interference. Since income tax records reveal personal financial information, any income tax system can potentially lead to unwarranted public exposure or government abuse. Land deeds, on the other hand, don't need to be hidden from public view since they don't reveal any private financial information; land contributions will be based entirely on property records, which are already publicly available.

Furthermore, because land-value data will be publicly available, land users will be able to compare their land's assessed rental value with the assessed rental values of their neighbors'; this practice effectively minimizes the potential for abuse and government corruption. Should land users feel that the assessed rental value of the land they use is too great, they can appeal to a local land-value assessment board, as property owners today can appeal their real-estate taxes to property tax assessment boards.

In addition to *efficient*, *simple*, and *transparent*, a public revenue system also needs to be *fair* in order to be truly effective. If the system isn't innately fair and just, it will inevitably create a wide variety of problems that are difficult to address and cost society enormous amounts of wasted resources. One of the most prevalent forms of taxation in effect today is the so-called *progressive income tax*—a tax by which the wealthy are taxed on their income at a greater percentage rate than the less affluent. Although such a tax perhaps appears fair, especially from the perspective of those who live on a lower income, the progressive income tax isn't a fair tax at all.

Public revenues pay for a wide variety of public services, including infrastructure, police and fire protection, and public schooling. Public services provide real and tangible benefits to society, benefits that are local to the areas that they service; in other words, many public services add value to neighborhoods, which is really just another way of saying that they add value to land. For example, realtors know that properties in neighborhoods with good public school systems and better public transportation options tend to be more expensive than properties in neighborhoods with lower-quality schools or that don't have good access to public transportation. And since public revenues pay for these public services, they ultimately end up increasing land values and thus reward those who *own property* (the wealthy) to the detriment of those who do not (the less affluent). Any tax that pays for public services without obtaining revenue from resulting land-value increases is fundamentally unjust.

In 2006, Fred Harrison—the aforementioned economist who wrote about the eighteen-year real-estate cycle—claimed in his book *Ricardo's Law: House Prices and the Great Tax Clawback Scam* that property owners (taken together as a whole) are generally able to recoup their cumulative income tax payments through gains made from land values, while renters are financially penalized through their income taxes.[56] Harrison goes on to claim that even the progressive income tax is therefore a great orchestrated tax scam by which the poor are effectively forced to subsidize the lifestyles of the rich.

Whether we consider our current income tax system to have been intentionally implemented to serve the interests of the wealthy at the expense of the poor, or whether we attribute our present-day situation to mere ignorance on part of those who institute and perpetuate the system, it's clear that our current tax system is inherently unfair.

MEDIA 9-3: RICARDO'S LAW: HOUSE PRICES AND THE GREAT TAX CLAWBACK SCAM

Video introduction to the book *Ricardo's Law: House Prices and the Great Tax Clawback Scam* by Fred Harrison. Ricardo's Law points lawmakers, policy analysts, and social reformers toward a model of public finances that's fair and able to deliver prosperity to everyone.

http://unitism.co/clawbackscam

Community land contributions are economically fair because they simply reclaim what never exclusively belonged to individuals to begin with. They're based on the *benefit principle*, according to Foldvary, since they reimburse communities for the benefits land users receive from using land in certain locations. Since public services provide benefits over a given area, community land contributions in effect *recycle* the value of these benefits back into the public purse. In other words, with community land contributions *we pay for what we receive*.

Community land contributions have other benefits that make them a truly fair source of public revenue. In "The Ultimate Tax Reform," Foldvary states that if land users can't pay their land contributions in full for whatever reason, they can defer their land contributions by accumulating liens on the land until they die or transfer the property, as is commonly done today with real-estate taxes. Land contributions, furthermore, are also immune to the practice of tax evasion: Foldvary explains that "nobody would be sent to prison for tax evasion, because there would be no tax evasion. A nonpayer would lose title to his land or lose the protective services of government, depending on the local enforcement practice. Without audits, bank account seizures, and fear-inspiring letters from the IRS requesting information or additional payments or imposing interest and penalties, the opportunity for tyranny would greatly diminish, if not entirely disappear. Evasion being impossible, there would be no need or excuse for any inquisitive state investigators of fraud." Unwarranted government intrusion is a danger to be reckoned with: Tax-collection agencies have the power to freeze bank accounts, garnish wages, and impose steep penalties and high interest rates (whether justified or not), among other powers. Due to their simplicity and transparency, community land contributions, on the other hand, don't offer opportunities for unwarranted government intrusion upon civil liberties.

But most of all, community land contributions are both ethical and economically fair because they allow people to keep the fruits of their labor. Land contributions charge people for what they *take away from other human beings*, not for *the value they provide* through their labor and their provisioning of capital goods. Since land contributions pay for the benefits we receive from society, and since communities give land its value, revenues from land contributions are the most logical primary income stream for any community.

And finally, let's consider whether land contributions provide *sufficient revenue*. Nature can abundantly provide for all of our needs. To realize this, we only need to observe the simple fact that all material wealth can only come about because of nature in the first place. The scarcity we've created only exists because we are monopolizing nature, and this scarcity requires governments to impose taxes.

The United States has a landmass of approximately 2.3 billion acres, of which nearly 60 percent, or 1.35 billion acres, is privately owned.[57] The sheer value of this land is nearly incomprehensible: Economist Mason Gaffney estimates the annual revenue that could be had from land in the United States at approximately $5.3 trillion dollars, which is what the United States collected in taxes in 2013.[58] And considering the inefficiencies that our current tax system creates, a shift away from taxes would increase revenues from land even more. If we also collected oil, gas, and mineral rents in addition to land values, these combined revenues could provide substantial, if not sufficient, revenue streams for the entire nation. Even if we begin by reclaiming greater amounts of land values while decreasing taxes on production and consumption, the efficiency gains of our economy could diminish, if not eliminate, our need for taxes altogether.

10. LOCAL AUTONOMY

*Each blade of grass has its spot on Earth whence it draws its
life, its strength; and so is man rooted to the land from which
he draws his faith together with his life.*

—Joseph Conrad (1857–1924)

"I bear no enmity towards the English but I do towards
their civilization," said Mohandas K. Gandhi, known as
Mahatma or Great Soul due to his indomitable will and
selfless devotion to the people of India as he led them toward independence from British colonial rule. Although
he referred to the English civilization in this statement,
Gandhi was criticizing the social structures and institutions of so-called *dominator civilizations* in general. Dominator civilizations are characterized by people who don't
recognize that their own well-being depends upon the
well-being of the communities in which they live. As a
result of their sense of alienation, people within those
civilizations seek to control and dominate others, usually
through social structures that wield power from top to
bottom. Gandhi believed that as long as the autonomy
and freedom of each member of society is restricted, insti-
tutionalized violence will invariably pervade society. He
advocated the principle of *self-rule*, or *swaraj*, as an effective antidote to the globalized powers that often serve the

limited self-interests of private individuals, corporations, and governments.

Swaraj, according to Gandhi, is an acknowledgment of each human being's innate autonomy; it emphasizes individual self-reliance in both private and public affairs as an essential prerequisite to the experience of social unity and harmony on a larger scale. *Swaraj* challenges the belief that society can only be effectively managed from the top down, instead of on a local level from the ground up. The vision of *swaraj* is one in which local communities are effectively self-governing entities, yet also connected in their relationships to other sovereign communities around them. The principle of *swaraj* has been expressed in many shapes and forms throughout history. Just as it's intuited by modern political commentators in their calls for small government, it's also implicitly recognized by local grassroots advocacy groups and community-building endeavors.

But society today appears to be headed in the opposite direction. The lack of affordable access to land forces some of us to perform work that doesn't necessarily contribute to our local community and that has little to do with our unique abilities, interests, and desires to make a difference in the world; meanwhile, opportunities for self-employment and the honing of traditional crafts uniquely suited to our individual temperaments seem to diminish over time. Why are we witnessing this monumental shift in human development toward an ever-increasing centralization of power and top-down decision making? Is it just because our world has become increasingly interconnected through infrastructure and technology, or is there perhaps another, deeper reason?

We've observed that public revenue systems create behavioral incentives that directly influence individual as well as collective human destinies. Unfortunately, in most nations, tax revenues on production and consumption activities collected at the local level are often funneled straight to the national level, and from the national level they're then slowly redistributed back down to the local level. Income and payroll taxes, for example, are usually collected by the national government, but then only slowly find their way back into the local economy. This trickle-down approach encourages the centralization of power in two ways.

First, because tax revenues are not retained at the local level before they're redirected up toward the state and the national levels, wealth and power become concentrated in the hands of a few key decision makers. People in these positions of power are often able to divert great amounts of wealth for purposes of self-interest or the benefit of lobbying efforts, rather than for the benefit of the communities that created the wealth originally.

Second, if and when tax revenues find their way back down to the local level, they do so at only a fraction of the wealth originally siphoned off and usually come with strings attached. This practice not only creates unhealthy dependencies between local communities and higher levels of government, which are contrary to the democratic spirit, but also forces local communities to struggle for access to much-needed wealth that was theirs to begin with.

Just as Gandhi recognized that a top-down approach is generally detrimental to individuals, we too are wise to recognize that societies can only flourish over time as long as human beings remain empowered on a local level. To move forward, then, we need to consider the wisdom of *swaraj*—the wisdom of self-rule and local autonomy: We'll only be fully empowered on a local level if our money flows up instead of down. Locally generated wealth has to *first be retained* on the local level before it is passed up toward a city, state, national, and then an international level. Community land contributions have the potential to achieve this bottom-up approach. Since all wealth comes from nature, revenues from community land contributions can become the primary mechanism by which to retain wealth on a local level in a most efficient, empowered, and effective way.[59]

Land-use rights (see Chapter 8, Restoring Communities) are an effective way for wealth to be retained at a local level, since communities receive a perpetual income from properties tied to land-use rights. This model is markedly different from our current reality, where every time a property is sold, financial institutions provide financing to buyers who have to pay higher prices as land becomes more expensive over time. Through this process, community wealth is privatized and siphoned off by the financial sector and by property owners. Land-use rights, on the other hand, would counteract this tendency because land-use rights drastically lower the selling price of land; buyers would require little outside financing, if any, to purchase properties tied to land-use rights.

11. AFFORDABLE HOUSING

There can be no fairness or justice in a society in which some live in homelessness, or in the shadow of that risk, while others cannot even imagine it.

—Jordan Flaherty,
Community Organizer and Journalist

We live in a world of abundance yet simultaneous poverty. We can no longer blame famine, war, or lack of technological progress for the poverty that remains an inextricable part of human experience. Nor can we blame a debt-based monetary system alone for our state of affairs. Although money buys power, it can only do so, by and large, in an economic system in which wealth cannot easily be created due to the ownership and hoarding of land. Human beings need land even more so than they need money; the monopoly of land—not the monopoly of money—is the primary driver of poverty and inequality.[60] Once we understand that the issue is lack of *affordable access to land*, and therefore *to community*, we understand why the value of land has to be shared.

Economists worldwide have already laid much of the scientific groundwork for the effectiveness and validity of community land contributions. People unfamiliar with land contributions often wonder if these contributions will raise the cost of housing. However, as we shall see in this chapter, land actually becomes more affordable because land will no longer be hoarded. And since revenues from land contributions will diminish or even eliminate the need for conventional taxes, goods and services will become significantly more affordable. The end result is that homeowners are likely to incur net savings due to diminished or eliminated taxes and considerably lower costs of living.

Community land contributions only burden property owners who don't put land to efficient use. Tenants are unaffected because tenants *already* pay for the benefits they receive from the communities they're living in, except that they're paying their landlords instead of their communities. In other words, since tenants already pay land contributions to property owners, land contributions are already included in landlords' profits if they rent their properties out; if property owners try to pass community land contributions on to their tenants, and thus charge tenants *twice* for the community benefits tenants receive, they'll find that the property rental market will simply accommodate the tenant with another property owner who's willing to accept less of a profit.[61]

Nevertheless, community land contributions provide a win-win for everyone, since real-estate developers can still gain from the value of the housing they provide; they just won't be able to profit as much from land anymore. And because community land contributions will lead to an overall increase in wealth for society while preventing a greater increase in the cost of living, community land contributions are extremely beneficial for tenants as well.

Our current laws and practices don't support the dream of affordable housing for the average person. Meanwhile, homeowners with expensive mortgages are burdened by their liabilities; our current system doesn't easily allow them to sell their homes and rent instead. Flawed economic policies meant to encourage homeownership—and thereby land ownership—are rotten at their core because they're built on the assumption that land ought to be owned and profited from. As a result, such policies gear us to consider short-term self-interest at the expense of common interests, and therefore at the expense of our own long-term self-interest.

One way for communities to create affordable housing is for local communities to adopt land-use rights. To accomplish a transition toward such a model, either local governments or community land trusts would provide financing to homebuyers, who would then make land contributions on their properties in perpetuity. As a result, communities would get reimbursed for the goods and services they provide to homeowners, while property buyers would primarily become *home* buyers, not *land* buyers. This way, the price of real estate can potentially decrease anywhere from 10 to 70 percent, depending on the conditions of the local real-estate market, and everyone wins.

Let's use a practical example: If a property sells for $250,000 but has a house on it that's valued at $100,000, we know that the property's land (or location) value is $150,000. Accordingly, a homebuyer of a $250,000 property pays a premium of $150,000 just for the privilege of living in a certain community. That premium, however, doesn't flow into the pockets of the community in which this property is located: The previous owners as well as the financial institutions that have provided financing along the way have pocketed this premium instead.[62]

Let's take our example a bit further: Two people, John and Susan, each decide to buy a condominium in that location for $250,000. For the sake of simplicity, let's assume both John and Susan make a down payment of $50,000, or 20 percent, toward the property. To pay for the $200,000 remainder, John opts for a thirty-year mortgage at an interest rate of 5 percent, while Susan opts for a land-use right. Her local community, in order to promote affordable housing, provides Susan with $120,000 in cash for the property's location value as well as a thirty-year mortgage at an interest rate of 5 percent for the remainder of $80,000 in exchange for issuing Susan a land-use right.[63]

As soon as Susan buys the property—now tied to a land-use right—the property's selling price decreases significantly, because whoever owns this property from now on is forevermore obligated to make a community land contribution based on the location value of this property. So while John's condominium continues to be priced at $250,000, Susan's condominium is now priced at only $140,000, *a reduction of 44 percent.*[64] Meanwhile, John pays a total of $1,036 per month in mortgage interest and property taxes during the first year; Susan, however, only pays a total of $731 per month in mortgage interest and land contributions.

Let's take a look at the money flow for the next ten years. Whenever land is bought and sold, three stakeholders automatically vie for a cut from the revenue that can be had from land: the *community*, the *property owner*, and the *institutions that finance property ownership*. When land increases in value, these increases are always distributed among those three stakeholders, depending upon how the value of land is divided.

Assuming an average land-value growth rate of 2 percent per year and a general interest rate of 3 percent, a $250,000 condominium with no land-use right might cost $283,000 in ten years. A land-use right property, however, will still only be priced at $149,000, even after ten years. The advantages to future homebuyers immediately become apparent: With real-estate prices once again affordable, new homeowners can put their money to other uses instead. Meanwhile, land contributions for this property will have increased from $400 per month to about $478 per month (community land contributions generally tend to increase over time the more a city grows).[65]

John pays a total of $897 per month in mortgage interest and property taxes during the tenth year, while Susan makes combined mortgage interest and land contribution payments of $753 per month (see Table 11-1).

TABLE 11-1: MONTHLY COST OF LIVING COMPARISON FOR THE TENTH YEAR

	John	Susan
Mortgage interest	$ (688)	$ (275)
Property tax	$ (208)	$ 0
Land contribution	$ 0	$ (478)
Cost of Living	$ (897)	$ (753)

In John's case the bank will take the lion's share of the land value via mortgage interest payments. With land-use rights, meanwhile, the community will be much better off: The revenue collected on behalf of the community during those ten years comes to about $53,000, more than twice of $25,000, which is what the community would have otherwise collected in property taxes (see Table 11-2).

TABLE 11-2: TOTAL EXPENSES DURING TEN YEARS

	John	Susan
Mortgage interest	$ (91,521)	$ (36,609)
Property tax	$ (25,000)	$ 0
Land contribution	$ 0	$ (52,559)
Cost of Living	$ (116,521)	$ (89,167)

In order for our land-contribution model to be complete, we have to consider two more aspects in our affordable-housing discussion. First, we have to minimize the inequality between tenants and landowners, and second, we have to provide the landless—the homeless—with guaranteed access to land.

Currently, property owners can profit from land while tenants cannot. Because tenants aren't able to profit from land, they usually end up being gentrified out when rents increase. Unfortunately, in our current economic model there are few things communities can do short of implementing rent control to prevent rents from increasing; higher rents are a natural byproduct of increased affluence for a given area. Because this affluence is only pocketed by property owners and financial institutions and not shared with all residents, rent control often seems like the least bad option in the fight against gentrification. But rent control comes with a host of negative side effects, including a shortage of housing and lower-quality housing, and doesn't serve the community in the long run.[66]

What's required is an entirely new mechanism by which higher rents are shared with all residents—property owners and tenants alike. One effective way to do this is through the issuance of a partial *Universal Basic Income* to all residents, financed entirely from community land contributions. A Universal Basic Income, only when exclusively derived from community land contributions, has the effect of preventing gentrification: When tenants receive a Universal Basic Income, they're able to afford the higher rents, which they pay to their landlords, who in turn have to pay more money to their local community and provide better services to their tenants. The community, in turn, then shares that added revenue with all community members—and everyone wins.

Having one's own home can tremendously ease one's mind in a way that few other things in life can; the homeless are often painfully aware of this reality because they lack that psychological security. While some people tend to believe that the homeless are either lazy or mentally incapable of earning enough money to afford a place to live, few people consider the principle that land has to be shared with *all* human beings—regardless of whether a person contributes to society or not. This is because no human being has made land; therefore no human being has a justifiable right to marginalize another person from land. Furthermore, all of us need land, just like we need air to breathe.

Since everyone has a basic right to land, it's society's duty to provide a minimum standard of free land access to all its members. It can do this for property owners and tenants by providing them with a Universal Basic Income; the homeless, however, should also be given the option of free public housing (the cost of which can be deducted from their Universal Basic Income share) so that they can have accommodations without living in fear of being evicted. To provide the homeless with free housing also makes sense on a financial basis, since the cost of providing housing for the homeless often tends to be significantly less than the actual welfare costs and societal burdens that are created by homelessness.[67]

Land is a universal human right. Consider how important it is for the human mind to have a ground to call its own! But in order for everyone to have their own ground, the value of land has to be shared, and housing has to be provided to those who live on the margins.

Land belongs to the people, yet the homeless are not only homeless—they are landless. Their poverty is less a reflection of their inability to sufficiently provide for themselves in a predatory economic system, and much more a reflection of our collective ignorance. Once we realize that everyone has a right to land—and therefore, to shelter—and once we realize how we commoditize this right to the highest bidder, it becomes apparent how we each are complicit in each other's poverty. It is therefore up to all of us to do our part in alleviating poverty and creating, in the words of Charles Eisenstein, "the more beautiful world our hearts know is possible."

12. THRIVING CITIES

Rent is not a tax. It is payment for the use of a location, determined by the higgling and haggling of the market, and it makes no difference to the land user whether he pays rent to the city fathers or to a private owner.

—Frank Chodorov (1887–1966)

Imagine a man who works very hard and makes valuable contributions at his place of employment every day. At the end of each week, just as he's about to get paid in recognition of the value he created on behalf of his employer, he refuses his paycheck and tells his employer that he has been, in fact, spending several hours at the end of each workday begging for money on the street. This, he says, is how he prefers to earn an income. As strange as we might consider this man's behavior to be, he would be acting just like city governments all around the world today. City governments provide indispensable services to residents and commuters—the people who keep them employed— yet are inadequately compensated for their services, and in ways that are largely unrelated to the value they create through the services they provide.

Whenever a city offers better services, such as increased police protection or public transportation, the value of land in the areas that are positively affected by the presence of these additional services usually increases, often significantly.[68] Property owners are able to pocket the property-value gains caused by these added services, while cities struggle to find sufficient revenue sources to cover their mounting expenses. City governments tend to reclaim only small portions of the values that their services create for property owners; they usually attempt this by applying a property tax. While property taxes capture some of the value that city services provide—though only to a small extent—they also contain taxes on building values and therefore penalize both existing homeowners and commercial real-estate developers alike. A property tax, therefore, is a mixed bag. Land speculators, developers, and rentiers (those who live on income from property or investments), many of whom make money without providing goods or services of corresponding value, often wield considerable power in city halls and tend to oppose community land contributions, so cities have generally found it difficult to abolish the property tax in favor of pure community land contributions.

In a bid to bridge the gap between the property tax and land contributions, some forward-thinking cities in the United States and other parts of the world have already instituted a two-tier property tax, also known as *a split-rate property tax*: They first separate the value of a property's improvements from the value of a property's underlying land, then they apply one tax rate to the value of improvements and another to the value of the underlying land. Then, over time, they gradually *decrease* the tax rate on the value of improvements and *increase* the rate on the value of land. This process allows homeowners and commercial real-estate developers to experience a gradual transition toward a system in which they increasingly pay for the benefits they receive through their exclusive use of land. This transition creates healthier economic incentives for both homeowners and commercial real-estate developers over time.

MEDIA 12-1: HOW PENNSYLVANIA CITIES GOT THE TWO-RATE PROPERTY TAX

From Rick Rybeck and Walt Rybeck, published in Public Management Magazine, August 2012, vol. 94, no. 4.

http://unitism.co/splitratetax

The property tax is one of the closest approximations we have today to community land contributions. For this reason, property tax rates and home-affordability rates—which is to say, *land*-affordability rates—are inversely correlated: The lower the property tax, the more expensive, on average, the property.[69] When property owners pay lower property taxes, they end up paying less money to society for their use of land. The problem, however, is that since lower property taxes tend to increase the selling price of land, ironically property owners generally end up paying more money for land overall—not to society, but to other landowners and financial institutions that finance property ownership.

The havoc that lower property taxes wreak on society has been demonstrated clearly in the state of California: In 1978 California voters passed Proposition 13 by popular vote, which limited property taxes to only 1 percent of the total home value. Proposition 13 also artificially revalued the property tax base to what it was worth in 1975 and stipulated that the *assessed*, as opposed to the *actual*, property tax base couldn't increase by more than 2 percent per year. Furthermore, Proposition 13 mandated that the property tax base wouldn't be reassessed annually, but only upon new construction or change of property ownership. The overall intent of the legislation was to minimize the tax exposure of long-term homeowners by keeping property tax rates as well as assessed property values artificially low; in this regard, Proposition 13 succeeded all too well. Unfortunately, and as a predictable side effect, land prices in California have skyrocketed because land became a prime mechanism by which property owners—and financial institutions profiteering from mortgages—were able to deplete social wealth.

MEDIA 12-2: FREE RIDERS ON PUBLIC TRANSPORT

The construction of the Jubilee line illustrates how public efforts benefit property owners and what can be done about it. This is an excerpt from the documentary Real Estate 4 Ransom, which outlines how economics have been sculpted to allow such enormous leakages to flow into the pockets of a fortunate few.

http://unitism.co/freeridersvideo

Lobbyists for Proposition 13 promised California voters that California public schools, which at that time received much of their funding from property tax revenues, would benefit from the passing of the legislation. This, of course, turned out to be a false claim; soon after the passing of Proposition 13, California's once-prized educational system not only lost a significant portion of its funding, but also decreased in quality to such an extent that today it measures near the bottom in the United States overall in terms of student performance. Schools, once largely self-reliant for funding, now increasingly depend upon financial assistance from the State of California (observe the phenomenon of trickle-down tax revenues mentioned in Chapter 10, Local Autonomy), while cities and counties throughout California are faced with significantly lower tax revenues resulting from property tax limitations. And because lower property taxes lead to higher land values, California property owners end up paying more money for land overall; this vicious cycle makes Proposition 13 even more unfair to California homeowners and taxpayers alike.

MEDIA 12-3: PROPOSITION 13'S IMPACT ON SCHOOLS

Is Proposition 13 to blame for California's near-bottom per-pupil funding in the country? Gloria Penner and Joanne Faryon of San Diego's KPBS discuss the impact that Proposition 13 has had on the funding of California's school system.

http://unitism.co/prop13impact

There are a number of other reasons why land contributions are necessary to the vitality of every town, city, and metropolitan area. Urban sprawl, for example, is the symptom of a wasteful use of space—of land. But land is a precious commodity, particularly in desired locations. Therefore, it's essential to give land users and real-estate developers proper economic incentives to encourage them to use land efficiently. Our current economic system allows people to own empty lots in valuable locations. Often, such lots appreciate more in value than what they cost in property taxes. The result is that property owners and real estate developers are aren't incentivized to put land to good use—even as they prevent other people from using it at the same time! But when the use of every inch of land comes at an ongoing cost to land users, land users are forced to use land efficiently, which is why charging entities for land use has the potential to inhibit urban sprawl.

Many cities are currently experimenting with other methods to inhibit urban sprawl, such as urban-growth boundaries, also known as greenbelts. Urban-growth boundaries, however, cause urban land prices to skyrocket because land is made even scarcer than it already is. As developers are pressured into using up all available space for development, cities are likely to have taller buildings where less tall buildings would have been entirely sufficient, as well as even fewer open spaces such as parks and other amenities. This pressure can also cause development to jump over the greenbelt and create so-called *satellite towns*, which often operate more like commuter suburbs rather than independent communities. On the other hand, if we lived in a world where people paid their communities for their use of land, suburban sprawl wouldn't exist because every inch of land would have an ongoing cost. We would live in a world where we would only have several large, sustainable cities surrounded by farms, with plenty of untouched green spaces in between.

Charging people a fair market rent for their use of land encourages the efficient organization of any town, city, and metropolis; at the same time, it keeps land prices in check relative to the wealth it generates for the area to which it is applied. Community land contributions lead to a more intensive use of land and encourage the greening of a city's surroundings, as the existing population will tend to cluster closer together. Land contributions also have a tendency to encourage the restoration of blighted urban areas.[70] With more and more people living in cities, isn't it important that we enhance the quality of life in urban areas? If we share the value of land, urban sprawl and poverty, with all their costly side effects and social drawbacks, no longer need to be automatic byproducts of urban areas. Ultimately, however, if we want to achieve true and lasting sustainability, all city land eventually has to be owned by the community. Private land use can then easily be accommodated through the implementation of tradable land-use rights; in this way, banks no longer make money off of land and people no longer have to clamor for land access.

MEDIA 12-4: MY GREEDY GENERATION

In this video, economist Mason Gaffney, professor of economics at the University of California, Riverside, talks about the major reason for urban sprawl and suburban dystopia. Can America turn around the social and economic problems that are now beyond the control of federal and state governments? Dr. Gaffney argues that effective solutions have to be underpinned by a radical reform of the tax system.

  http://unitism.co/mygreedygen

13. SUSTAINABLE FARMING

The men of olden times believed that above all moderation should be observed in landholding, for indeed it was their judgment that it was better to sow less and plow more intensively. To confess the truth, the latifundia [large landed estates] have ruined Italy, and soon will ruin the provinces as well.

—Pliny the Elder (AD 23–AD 79)

One of the many concerns people have about community land contributions is their impact on agriculture. After all, farmers, ranchers, and horticulturalists depend upon their extensive and productive use of land for their livelihood. The concern is that they may be unable to afford the land they cultivate. But this perception is based upon a misunderstanding of farmland contributions, which are merely payments for the benefits that farmers receive from their land and from working near communities; they don't impinge upon any of the wealth that farmers generate through their enterprise (net profits are apt to significantly increase with the removal of taxes on productive endeavors). Also, farmland contributions tend to be comparatively low by default, since farmland tends to be much more affordable than urban land. Farmland contributions encourage large acreages of land that have been previously withheld from the market and not put to productive use to once again become available. More available farmland, in turn, leads to even lower farmland contributions. In addition, food production itself can become more sustainable since the cost of production inputs such as labor, supplies, and machinery will be reduced while the demand for goods is likely to increase due to the absence or reduction of conventional taxes.

In our current distorted reality, land is often held speculatively without being put to productive use. As a result, agricultural land today often bears a speculative value based on the belief that it will be used in the future for urban purposes. Because people are able to profit from land, suburban sprawl has become a major issue; towns and cities use up significantly more land than they really need. This causes the value of farmland to increase. Because of these artificial wealth distortions, certain artificial legal interventions, such as agricultural zoning laws and tax breaks, have become increasingly necessary to prevent farmland from being converted to urban use.

Urban sprawl also entices older farmers priming for their retirement to cash out by selling their farms to urban developers in order to fund their retirement. This dynamic, in turn, incentivizes urban developers to apply pressure on local authorities to change zoning ordinances—a practice that's obviously unsustainable but nonetheless encouraged under our current system.[71] According to the U.S. Department of Agriculture, *half* of all current farmers are likely to retire by the year 2020;[72] they will leave the next generation of farmers with nearly insurmountable hurdles, chief among them being the elevated price of land. In a poll of 1,300 young and aspiring farmers from across the U.S. conducted by the National Young Farmers Coalition, an advocacy organization for young farmers, 78 percent of respondents cited a lack of funds while 68 percent specifically cited lack of land access as preventing them from successfully owning and operating a farm.[73] In the face of these challenges, isn't it evident that less and less farmland will become available to a younger generation of independent farmers, despite their need for farmland in their quest to provide food for society? And with more farmland used for speculative purposes instead of for food production, won't more and more of the available land remain concentrated in the hands of those with plenty of access to money, such as large agribusinesses and Wall Street investors?

MEDIA 13-1: TENNESSEE FARMLAND PROTECTION LAW SHELTERS TAXES FOR RICH AND FAMOUS

Nationally, preferential tax laws benefiting farming are abused by businesspeople holding land for development, despite scant evidence the programs actually prevent development.

http://unitism.co/farmlandtaxshelter

Because farmland contributions will never be greater than the cost to lease farmland on the open market (excluding the value of improvements), and because the rental value of farmland will always be at a rate at which hardworking and efficient farmers can profit, farmland contributions guarantee profits for those who know how to use land efficiently. According to another study by the U.S. Department of Agriculture, a staggering 29 percent of all farmland in 2007 was owned by landlords who leased to tenant farmers.[74] If tenant farmers can succeed even now with taxes on labor and capital, clearly owner-occupants can succeed as well, even when they are unable to profit from farmland itself. Tenant farmers, too, will succeed in an economy based on land contributions because they've already proven their ability to pay for their use of land—except that they will now have to pay their communities instead of their landlords. Farmland contributions won't negatively impact tenant farmers because land contributions, as we've discovered in Chapter 11, Affordable Housing, can't be passed on from landlords to tenants. With farmland contributions, farmers will only lose money if they use land below its productive potential. Farmland contributions—as a fraction of the market rental value of farmland—always guarantee a profit for those who use farmland well.

In order to help us better understand this dynamic, let's again consider the example in Chapter 3, The Free Market, a scenario in which we own an unimproved plot of land that we can either rent out on the open market for $6,000 per year, or, alternatively, use for our own purposes. In that example, we choose to use it for our own purposes and hire a part-time farmer who generates a total of $20,000 worth of produce. We pay the farmer $9,000 in wages and purchase equipment for $3,000. We realize, however, that due to our outright ownership of land, we're able to profit from land by pocketing its *rent* (Table 3-1, Farm Profit).

With our newfound knowledge, let's consider this scenario again, but this time let's analyze several other factors. At present, incomes are taxed, while land can be owned outright, so let's use an income tax rate of 20 percent, which gives us an income tax of $1,600 (20 percent of $8,000, our gross profit), as well as a property tax of $1,500, and compare it to an 80 percent land-contribution rate, which gives us a land contribution of $4,800 (80 percent of $6,000, the land's rental value). For illustrative purposes, the precise rates we use aren't nearly as significant as the general implications we can derive from how increases and decreases to our numbers affect our profit and loss calculations.

What happens if we *increase* our income tax rate as well as the land contribution? If we gradually increase our income tax rate, income taxes will gradually eat into the wealth generated by our labor and hard work until nothing remains. If, however, we gradually increase our land contribution so that it approximates even more of the rental value of land, any additional wealth produced with our labor and ingenuity remains untouched, since land contributions always remain at or below the rental value of the land, in this case $6,000.

Clearly the farmer is better off with a combined income tax and property tax payment of $3,100 rather than with a land contribution of $4,800. But is she really? Another important financial factor plays into the profit and loss equation: High land values lead to greater financing costs for those unable to purchase land outright, while those able to purchase land without a mortgage by definition have less money to spend on production (since they used their money to buy land). Either way, elevated land prices prevent the optimal use of money, which affects a farmer's bottom line.

Let's continue the previous example in which we have income and property taxes of $3,100 and land contributions of $4,800. Since we know the land's rental value, assuming a rate of return of 3 percent and a property tax rate of 1 percent, we can approximate the purchase price of this land to be about $150,000 (see the Appendix, The Math behind the Science, for more details). If we apply a land contribution of $4,800 per year on the use of this land and remove the property tax, the land's purchase price is likely to diminish to about $40,000, since the prospect of land contributions reduces the amount we're willing to pay out of pocket for land.

Let's assume that in both scenarios we purchased this land with a mortgage using a down payment of 20 percent at an interest rate of 5 percent. In an income tax and property tax scenario, high land values cause our yearly payment for a thirty-year mortgage on the outstanding balance to be about $5,960 for the first year, resulting in an annual net loss in spite of our productivity as a farmer. In a land-contribution scenario, however, land values are lower, and this greatly decreases what we owe the bank: Our financing costs average out to only about $1,589 annually, which still enables us to make a profit (see Table 13-2).

TABLE 13-2: FARM PROFIT AND LOSS

Tax Scenario		Land-Contribution Scenario	
Land value	$ 150,000	Land Value	$ 40,000
Down payment	$ (30,000)	Down payment	$ (8,000)
Mortgage principal	$ 120,000	Mortgage principal	$ 32,000
Gross profit	$ 8,000	Gross profit	$ 8,000
Financing	$ (5,960)	Financing	$ (1,589)
Principal payment	$ (1,770)	Principal payment	$ (472)
Income tax	$ (1,600)	Income tax	$ 0
Property tax	$ (1,500)	Property tax	$ 0
Land Contributions	$ 0	Land Contributions	$ (4,800)
Net Loss	$ (2,830)	Net Gain	$ 1,139

The point is clear: *The more money is tied up in land, the less people are able to support themselves through their contributions to society*. No wonder banks are so powerful in our economy! Of course, land contributions aren't likely to be welcomed by the financial and real-estate industries that continue to make a killing from the trade of land. These industries want to *keep real estate prices high*. If we consider that farmland contributions currently paid to private individuals and financial institutions for a profit represent a significant portion of farm expenses today, we quickly realize that land contributions can minimize farm expenses and greatly increase total farm profits.[75]

Toward the end of the nineteenth century in the United States, cattle ranchers owned vast amounts of land. Henry Miller, for example, was one of the most prominent landowners and cattle ranchers of his time: At one point he owned *over 1.4 million acres of land* and supposedly could drive his cattle from the Mexican border all the way up to Oregon and *spend every night on his own property!* Back then, much of the land that bordered California's lakes and rivers had been bought up by private landowners who charged farmers exorbitant fees for their use of water—a precious and scarce commodity in California—consequently putting many family farms out of business.

In 1887, the State of California passed the Wright Act, which allowed the creation of special water-irrigation districts. The cost to build the irrigation infrastructure was financed through the taxation of land, which actually rose in value as a result of increased irrigation and fertilization. Land became too costly to own for ranchers; consequently, they sold the land at affordable prices to farmers who were able to put the land to productive use. Within ten years, California's San Joaquin Valley transformed into a vast network of irrigated independent farms. A once-arid desert became the *"breadbasket of America,"* one of the most agriculturally productive areas on the planet.[76]

The moment we begin to share the value of land, farmland will once again become affordable; anyone with the skill and ability to efficiently grow food will be able to purchase or lease land from their local community at a significantly lower cost and turn a profit. Small family farms, which tend to use land efficiently, will once again have a viable chance at growing food for their local communities, empowering them in the process. Agricultural methods such as permaculture, which use land both intensively and harmoniously, are poised to thrive in this new economic paradigm.[77]

MEDIA 13-3: THE KILLING FIELDS

The Killing Fields is a documentary highlighting the importance that economics plays in wildlife conservation. The film explores the relationship between wildlife, land, economics, and law. It's presented by economist Fred Harrison and features Peter Smith, CEO and founder of the Wildwood Trust, Dr. Duncan Pickard, landowner and farmer, and Polly Higgins, environmental lawyer, author, and campaigner.

http://unitism.co/thekillingfieldsdoc

14. THE PRICE OF PEACE

Permanent peace can only be established when men and nations have realized that natural resources should be a common heritage, and used for the good of all mankind.

—First Viscount Philip Snowden (1864–1937)

There are, essentially, only three ways we can obtain wealth: We can *create* wealth, *receive it* from someone else, or *take it away* from someone else. In economics, the term *rent seeking* signifies a person's attempt to *take away* wealth, which the person can accomplish by manipulating the social and political environment in order to redirect the flow of income. Nobel laureate economist Joseph Stiglitz defined rent seeking as "using political and economic power to get a larger share of the national pie, rather than to grow the national pie."[78] In a sense, rent seeking is the seeking of privileged access to community wealth, which, of course, also includes the rent from land. Rent seeking is endemic to our civilization: It leads to a dysfunctional society based on exploitation and results in the corrosion of the social fabric. Individual exploitation leads to wealth inequality, cultural degeneration, and crime; ecological exploitation causes species extinction and habitat destruction; national exploitation fosters global insecurity and war. Nations, for example, engage in rent seeking whenever they covet resources abroad instead of using their own resources more efficiently and sustainably at home. Nations actively engaged in rent seeking are usually participating in an age-old practice known as land grabbing.

As a city may fail to make efficient use of its urban areas and instead expand into its surroundings in search of cheap land, a nation may choose to engage in rent seeking by acquiring ownership or control of foreign resources it considers of strategic interest. The reason that rent seeking on a national level works similarly to urban sprawl is because in both cases we are underutilizing preexisting resources: If a city grows, it either needs to use its land more efficiently by permitting the construction of additional and taller buildings within city boundaries, or sprawl onto neighboring land. Sprawling requires the city to invest additional capital—roads and other transportation infrastructures, as well as electric and sewer lines, for example. However, most cities don't regain their infrastructure investments by recouping the resulting rise in land values, so existing taxpayers are forced to foot the bill. Similarly, a nation engaged in the acquisition of foreign resources requires an expensive and sophisticated infrastructure of military, industrial, and commercial enterprises, which are, ultimately, financed by taxpayers at home.[79]

Any nation that seeks the acquisition of foreign resources is engaged in rent seeking. Maintaining an active empire infrastructure is a costly endeavor for any nation, and the gains from foreign resources generally only benefit a few, leading to a rise in domestic wealth inequality. Nations then fail to keep their home economies in good shape while they simultaneously overextend themselves abroad in ways that, given enough time, precipitate their eventual demise.

This process of rent seeking on a national level has expressed itself throughout human history: Nazi Germany's quest for *Lebensraum*, Europe's colonialism, America's *manifest destiny* as well as its waging of foreign wars, and China's acquisition of land in Africa and South America are all examples of rent seeking on a national level in one form or another. Rent-seeking behavior has also occurred on an individual level when landless peasants fleeing the high rents and poverty in Europe settled on other continents; new landlords on these continents couldn't charge as much rent because there was a vast expanse of quality land that settlers could own rent-free. The American Dream itself was only made possible because of the availability of cheap land—land that was taken from Native Americans.

It's also possible to counteract the tendency toward rent seeking on a global scale. Fred Foldvary conceives of a so-called *geo-confederacy*, a conflict mediation tool for nations engaged in territorial disputes based on historical, cultural, or political feuds. Under his proposal, land contributions are levied upon territorially disputed areas by an international conflict mediation agency set up particularly for that purpose (a *confederacy*). Land contributions are payable to the *confederacy* by the various nations that occupy the disputed territories in exact proportion to the land values of those territories. The *confederacy* then redistributes these funds back to the occupying nations as well as to the affected population within those territorially disputed areas. In this way, occupation over a disputed area comes with a price—a price that more accurately reflects the actual economic gains sought by the occupying nations, as well as the actual economic costs that are being inflicted upon the people in the disputed territories. Using one of the most historically difficult conflicts as an example—the Israeli-Palestinian conflict—Foldvary shares with us how a *geo-confederacy* might look:[80]

> Under a geo-confederacy, the governments of Israel and Palestine would own land at a price. At present, land held by either side now has no carrying cost. But if each had to pay dearly for each acre it holds, perhaps the price of holding it would induce a less intense desire to maximize land area and land value. The [*confederacy*] could, as an example, distribute 30 percent of the rent to the governments of the constituent states on the basis of their population. Another 30 percent of the rents could be paid equally to the two states, each getting 15 percent. This would act as a counterweight to a population war. The *confederacy* would retain the remaining land rent for its administration and the retirement of any debts or for agreed-on compensation for losses.

For the Israelis to accept a settlement, they need to regard it not as yielding territory, but changing its governance; not as a withdrawal, but an agreement to share sovereignty; not as the establishment of a hostile neighboring state, but as the preservation of Jewish autonomy within a common government over which they will have significant control.

The Palestinians are under pressure for a settlement. The economy of the Palestinian Authority has been devastated and cannot long endure the restrictions imposed by Israel in response to the continuing violence. But Palestinians, too, will nevertheless resist a settlement unless they see it as a just plan. Obtaining their share of the rent from all the land in Israel and Palestine as compensation for not possessing it would go a long way towards the perception of economic justice.

The ultimate source of resentment and hatred is the feeling that another is enjoying a privilege, an unfair advantage, or a position of dominance. When all are politically equal, such feelings would subside and then and only then would cooperation and friendship be possible. The political struggle for land would be transformed into an economic marketplace where those who use the land compensate the others for their use of their common homeland.

MEDIA 14-1: PEACE THROUGH CONFEDERAL DEMOCRACY AND ECONOMIC JUSTICE

In this paper, economist Fred Foldvary offers a proposal by which the rent of disputed territories are collected for public benefit as a way to accurately reflect the real cost of occupation.

http://unitism.co/globalconfederacy

Will we ever see such a resolution of the Israeli-Palestinian conflict? Ultimately, it depends upon the degree to which we are willing to sacrifice our own short-term self-interest on behalf of the greater good, which includes our long-term self-interest. Peace has a price, and that price is the unearned income we receive from land. As long as we are unwilling to share the value of land with one another, it's likely that we may not create enduring peace, no matter how hard we may try otherwise. But if we find within ourselves the willingness to share the gifts of nature with one another, we may stand a reasonable chance of finally attaining a lasting peace on Earth.

The price of peace is high because the changes we need to make are staggering; yet the price ultimately pales in comparison to the cost that all of us will have to bear if we refuse to share the Earth with one another. So let's resolve to pay the price of peace so that we may one day leave a lasting positive legacy for our children and our children's children.

15. A NEW PARADIGM

Our civilization is constitutionally incapable of reversing the annihilation of natural capital, or even slowing it down. Get used to that. When we really understand that, the project of reconceiving civilization itself will gain powerful impetus.

—Charles Eisenstein,
author of *The Ascent of Humanity*

When Oren Lyons, a Native American spokesman and faith keeper, attended the World Economic Forum in Davos, Switzerland, he challenged the assembled politicians and leaders of Fortune 100 companies—they were all men—to realize that their companies were destroying the Earth. One person in the audience, a CEO of a large company, responded that he was unable to reverse course since his company had to show a profit. If his company didn't show a profit, he said, he would be fired. "To whom must you show a profit?" Lyons asked. "To you, the stockholder," the man responded. "Are you married?" Lyons asked the CEO. "Yes, I am," he responded. "Do you have any grandchildren?" "Yes, I do; I have two boys." Then Lyons asked a key question: "When do you cease to be a CEO and start to become a grandfather?" Later, Lyons recalled, "There was a lot of silence there because that was a moral question. And if you don't have a moral question in your governing process, you don't have a process that's going to survive. That's the governing law. You must have a moral society, or you won't have any."[81]

Our industrialized culture is obsessed with economic growth: Investors, shareholders, CEOs, and politicians seek economic growth because our economic system demands it. But is economic growth what we really want? Once people reach a certain level of economic security, they generally tend to focus more on establishing meaningful relationships and activities that give them a sense of joy and fulfillment. Wouldn't we be wise to ask ourselves whether perpetual economic growth will truly enable us to fulfill our innermost desires? The answer to this question quickly becomes self-evident once we realize that economic growth in our current system simply perpetuates the very scarcity we seek to eradicate with more economic growth—the scarcity that prevents us from fulfilling our true desires in the first place.

Other efforts at resolving our social problems are also failing. For example, limiting population growth *on its own* cannot resolve today's social problems, since overpopulation is not the root cause of our social imbalance. A larger population that harmonizes with nature can live in greater balance with nature than a small population that consumes wastefully and destroys nature in the process.[82] But even so, with the human lifestyle the way it is, population growth remains a huge concern: It will eventually destroy our planet's fragile ecology if left unchecked.[83]

Equally, technological advancement in itself can't usher in an age of global prosperity. If technological progress makes certain areas more livable, those places become more attractive to live in, which increases demand for land there. Yet because the supply of land for each location is limited, land ends up becoming more expensive; technological progress thus also increases land values. Yet as long as the value of land isn't shared, land-value increases will prevent technological advancements from having a lasting positive impact for *all* members of society.

In our exploration, we've looked at some of the consequences that occur when we extract resources from local communities, and we've come across an entirely new paradigm that allows for a greater unfolding of human potential. Now, as we bring our journey to a close, we'll identify the process that has to occur in order for us to realize this new paradigm here on Earth.

The path to implementing this new paradigm is likely to be an arduous one, for change seldom comes easily. We human beings often tend to resist change, particularly if such change involves uncertainty. Yet change is what we're called upon to embrace, for as we each come in contact with this new paradigm and realize its potential to improve the quality of life for *all* human beings, we may come to realize that we hold in our hands an immensely powerful message of hope. Far from being a vague and impractical theory, we finally have a set of guidelines that harmoniously integrate our highest ideals and visions into a tangible and practical way of life—one that any community, town, city, state, or nation can freely live by.

The process of realizing this paradigm begins with *awareness*. When we each become sufficiently aware and realize how we affect one another, we begin to live in alignment with a worldview that is rooted in a deep connection to the living web of life around us. Awareness is followed by *education*: The more of us who understand how communities benefit whenever community-generated land values are shared with those that have created them, the more likely we will be able to successfully *advocate* for the implementation of this paradigm on a larger scale.[84]

Let's always remember that we each give birth to this new awareness. This paradigm requires a fundamental shift from seeing the individual self as a separate entity, cut off from the totality of life, toward recognition of the interdependency of all living things. When we sincerely ask, "What serves the highest good of all?" we evolve from resembling cancer cells, which multiply without regard for the rest of the body, to healthy cells in the body of life, aware of our interconnectedness. Anyone with a heart and mind that genuinely seeks out the common good can align themselves with a higher integrity in this way.

Our current economic and social structures are expressions of past choices made by individual human beings of diverse spans of consciousness. And because our consciousness tends to influence our surroundings as well as be influenced by it, our task is to transform not only ourselves but also the social structures that don't reflect our interdependency into functional and effective social structures that do. In this way, the realization of our interconnectedness can positively and increasingly affect everyone in society over time. But let's remember that it's up to each of us to do the necessary inner work first so that we can spread our new consciousness into our surroundings and mold our systems in new ways that remind us of our interconnectedness.

Education, our next step, is the process by which we raise awareness of this new paradigm, both within ourselves as well as in others. Because most of us treat land as property and don't recognize it as a gift to be shared, we usually don't think twice when real estate is bought and sold for a profit. We have to help homeowners realize that they have a right to profit from the financial value of their house, but not to the financial value of the land upon which that house exists.[85] However, unless offered attractive incentives, people are often resistant to change, and we'd be wise to include change incentives such as land-use rights as part of the education component. People are also more likely to embrace community land contributions once they realize that personal and corporate income, sales, and capital gains taxes aren't required in this new economic paradigm. Our task is to embed these change incentives into the public's awareness, for example through outreach programs. The ultimate aim of education is to help everyone recognize that it's truly in everyone's best interest to share the gifts of nature.

Legislative advocacy, the final step, can only succeed once a sufficient number of people have become aware of their interconnectedness as well as of this new paradigm. Once enough of us are aware, this paradigm stands a much better chance of being implemented on a legislative and political level.

But let's keep in mind that in order to create a world that works for all, we are first called upon to remember who we are as human beings, forever tied to the greater web of life. By undergoing this shift, we are changing the story of who we are in relationship to the planet we are living on and the beings we are living with. The more we live in alignment with this new awareness, the more we experience greater depth and purpose in our own lives and in our connections with others. The moment we open up, even briefly, to a genuine sense of this interconnectedness, we open up to an experience that's nothing short of wonder—a heartfelt sense of belonging and a knowledge that we're all in this together. Let's act from this place of remembrance so that we may positively affect our own well-being, the fate of our civilization, and the prosperity of generations to come.

EPILOGUE: A PERSONAL NOTE

*We do not inherit the Earth from our ancestors,
we borrow it from our children.*

—Native American proverb

Together we've explored the secret of how business cycles expand and contract, how we cannibalize nature, and how entire societies rise and fall. It is, like all good secrets, an ancient one; it has stood at the threshold of many revolutions, and has been endorsed by great thinkers throughout history. Although it seems almost forgotten today, its power endures: Truth is truth, even when denied, ignored, or scorned.

I spent many years looking for the hidden causes of our economic and ecological problems and then spent several more years researching for and writing this book. It contains wisdom that I believe is critical to the survival of the human race, as well as foundational to our hopes and dreams of leaving behind a better world for our children and our children's children.

During my childhood certain questions troubled me: Why do most people have so little, when a few have so much? And why don't the people who have more freely share with those in need? These questions preoccupied me on one level or another throughout my young life, which was why one of my childhood aspirations was to become someone who would share his possessions with those in need. As an adult I came to realize, however, that my youthful aspiration could neither help alleviate poverty on its own nor fill the pain of separation I felt inside. So instead I aimed to fulfill the deeper purpose of my childhood dream by simultaneously developing my own awareness and seeking out endeavors that might somehow help to create a more beautiful world.[86]

After graduating college, I set out to become an entrepreneur to see how society could be improved through social enterprise. In the process, I started paying close attention to the economic dynamics that helped influence the outcomes of my ventures. For example, I once co-managed a healing and community center, so location was crucial to our success; the landlord, however, commanded a substantial portion of our monthly earnings simply because he held a monopoly on our particular location, despite the fact that we were *already* paying taxes on incomes, payrolls, and sales. We were willing to pay for the benefits of a good location—just not twice. And since moving to another location would have brought with it the loss of locational advantage, I learned firsthand the extent to which landlords are able to extract unearned incomes from other people's contributions to society.

Over the years it occurred to me that the economic structure itself influences human beings in far more powerful ways than any single entrepreneurial venture ever could. I began to wonder if the state of the economy might be responsible for the destinies of entire nations. It was a profound realization: If the foundational structure of our economy were altered to better meet social needs, there could perhaps come a time when there would be little need for social enterprise or nonprofit work. *The economy itself could become one big enterprise for social good.*

My next challenge was to figure out what exactly in our economy needed to be changed, why, and how. I decided not to formally study mainstream economics since I intuited that its proponents had either not yet figured out a comprehensive and time-tested solution to poverty and wealth inequality, or didn't have the backbone to publicly advocate a position that might be politically controversial. I set about discovering for myself what *really* needed to be done in order to eliminate poverty and create a more prosperous world for everyone.

And so began a period of several years in which I researched various aspects of the economy. But my search provided no conclusive answer until I came across the Law of Rent. I immediately understood the essence of this principle and realized that the privatization of land values describes in basic terms how individuals and institutions profit from land at other people's expense. To learn more about this economic principle, I had to piece together my education from various sources; I couldn't find a single textbook that explained the entire topic in a comprehensive and simple way that I could understand. And so, over time, I realized that the work of explaining this topic, in a way that someone like me could understand, would fall to me.

I wrote *Land* both with the intent to understand and also to offer the world an economic solution that might soothe its many ills. However, the longer I studied this topic, the deeper I came to sense the pervasiveness of our collective ignorance. On a human level, I remain part of a collective story that seems bent on perpetuating the illusion of separation and disunity; my heart continues to be deeply affected when I see the desolate suffering among the homeless or witness financial struggle in daily life. It seemed appropriate to respond with compassion to the suffering we are causing one another and to do my little part to help us conceive of and create new social and economic systems. Consequently, I've embarked on the development of the Unitism concept—a sustainable alternative to our current form of capitalism. I'm inviting interested parties to join me in this effort by visiting the Unitism website at http://unitism.com.

Perhaps this book will open you up to new ideas on how to think and act to bring about a new humanity where all will thrive. It is my gift to the world. If you appreciate this work, please consider sharing your appreciation of it with others in a way that's meaningful to you.

My purpose in writing this book has now been fulfilled and the material has found its way into your hands: Take

it from here and run with it. I wish you well, my dear
fellow traveler on beautiful planet Earth.

APPENDIX

THE MATH BEHIND THE SCIENCE

Land prices are apt to change significantly with the introduction of community land contributions simply because land contributions prevent individuals and institutions from excessively profiting from land. While the following calculations offer us broad theoretical reference points, it isn't necessary to comprehend the math in order to understand the theory behind land contributions; the math is only mentioned here for the interested reader.

If P_{land} is the purchase price of land under a land-contribution system, i the prevailing interest rate, r the land's rental value, and c the contribution that is being collected, we use the following mathematical equation to estimate the new purchase price of land; for example, if i = 3%, r = $6,000, and c = $4,800, then:

$$P_{land} = \frac{(r-c)}{i} = \frac{(\$6,000-\$4,800)}{3\%} = \$40,000$$

The rental value of land—its rent r—can be approximated using the property tax–free purchase price of land P and the prevailing interest rate i, or the purchase price of land with a property tax P_{tax} (we'll assume a price of $150,000) along with the interest rate i and the property tax rate t (we'll assume a 1 percent property tax rate). This calculation is only an approximation, however, since purchase prices contain not only the capitalized rental value, but also include a speculative component as well (the speculative component will diminish the more land value is recovered):

$$r = P \times i = P_{tax} \times (i + t) = \$150,000 \times 4\% = \$6,000$$

Land contributions of $4,800 harness 80 percent of $6,000, the rental value of land. The formula to calculate this fraction f is:

$$f = c = \frac{\$4,800}{\$6,000} = 80\%$$

A property valued at $250,000 (with a land value of $150,000, a building value of $100,000, and a property tax rate of 1 percent) will be revalued at $140,000 (with a land value of $40,000 and a building value of $100,000) with a land contribution of $4,800 and no property tax—a 44 percent reduction.

REFERENCES AND SUGGESTIONS
FOR FURTHER READING

There are a number of resources that will further inform the reader about the economic science upon which this work is based; the following list contains materials that address in greater detail some of the topics covered in this work.

Alioto, Angela, et al. "The San Francisco Plan To Abolish Chronic Homelessness." June 30, 2004, San Francisco Mayor's Office of Housing and Community Development.

Andelson, Robert V., ed. *Commons without Tragedy: Protecting the Environment from Overpopulation—A New Approach.* London: Shepheard-Walwyn, 1991.

———*Land-Value Taxation Around the World: Studies in Economic Reform and Social Justice.* Malden, MA: Blackwell, 2000.

Arnott, Richard J., and Joseph E. Stiglitz. "Aggregate Land Rents, Expenditure on Public Goods, and Optimal City Size." *Quarterly Journal of Economics* 93, no. 4 (November 1979): 471–500.

Barnosky, Anthony D., Elizabeth A Hadly, Jordi Bascompte, Eric L. Berklow, James H. Brown, Mikael Fortelius, Wayne M. Getz, et al. "Approaching a State Shift in Earth's Biosphere." *Nature* 486 (June 2012): 52–58. http://www.nature.com/nature/journal/v486/n7401/full/nature11018.html.

Davis, Morris A. "Questioning Homeownership as a Public Policy Goal." Policy Analysis 696 (May 2012): 1–14. http://www.cato.org/publications/policy-analysis/questioning-homeownership-public-policy-goal.

Davis, Morris A., and Jonathan Heathcote. "The Price and Quantity of Residential Land in the United States," *Journal of Monetary Economics* 54, no. 8 (2007): 2595–620.

DeNardo, Gene. "A Critique of Murray Rothbard's Critique of the Georgist Argument." 2009. http://geoism.wikia.com/wiki/User:Gene09/A_Critique_of_Murray_Rothbard's_Critique_of_the_Georgist_Argument.

Duhigg, Charles, and Keith Bradsher. "How the U.S. Lost Out on iPhone Work." *New York Times*, January 22, 2012. http://www.nytimes.com/2012/01/22/business/apple-america-and-a-squeezed-middle-class.html.

Eisenstein, Charles. *The Ascent of Humanity.* Berkeley, CA: North Atlantic Books, 2013.

Foldvary, Fred E. "The Business Cycle: A Geo-Austrian Synthesis." *American Journal of Economics and Sociology* 56, no. 4 (1997): 521–41. http://onlinelibrary.wiley.com/doi/10.1111/j.1536-7150.1997.tb02657.x/abstract.

———"The Depression of 2026." *The Progress Report.* March 19, 2012. http://www.progress.org/2012/fold760.htm.

———"Peace through Confederal Democracy and Economic Justice." Accessed September 12, 2014. http://www.foldvary.net/works/globcon.html.

———"The Pre-existing Land Value Problem." *The Progress Report.* April 8, 2013. http://www.progress.org/2013/fold815.htm.

———*The Ultimate Tax Reform: Public Revenue from Land Rent.* Brochure, January 2006. http://www.foldvary.net/works/policystudy.pdf.

Friedman, Milton. "Milton Friedman, Land Value Tax and Internet Currencies." Filmed 1999. Accessed April 29, 2013. https://www.youtube.com/watch?v=j2mdYX1nF_Y.

Gaffney, Mason. "$5.3 Trillion Rent of the USA," YouTube video interview, published November 14, 2013, accessed March 15,

FURTHER READING

2014. https://www.youtube.com/watch?v=nLUGEMu9-sA

————"Benefits of Military Spending: An Inquiry into the Doctrine that National Defense Is a Public Good." Paper presented at the 10th Annual Conference, Committee on Taxation, Resources, and Economic Development, Madison, WI, March 1972. http://www.masongaffney.org/workpapers/1972_benefits_of_military_spending.pdf.

————"Causes of Downturns: An Austro-Georgist Synthesis." Working paper, 1982. http://www.masongaffney.org/workpapers/Causes_of_downturn—Austro-Georgist_synthesis_1982.pdf.

————"Rising Inequality and Falling Property Tax Rates," 1992. http://www.masongaffney.org/publications/D1Rising_Inequality_%26_Falling_Prop_Tax_Rates.CV.pdf.

————"The Taxable Capacity of Land." Published in Patricia Salkin, 1993. Land Value Taxation. Albany, NY: Government Law Center, Albany Law School, pp. 59-82.

Gaffney, Mason, and Fred Harrison. *The Corruption of Economics*. London: Shepheard-Walwyn, 2007.

George, Henry. *Progress and Poverty: An Inquiry into the Cause of Industrial Depressions and of Increase of Want with Increase of Wealth: The Remedy.* Garden City, NY: Doubleday, Page, 1879.

Harrison, Fred. *Boom Bust: House Prices, Banking and the Depression of 2010.* London: Shepheard-Walwyn, 2005.

————"Fred Harrison: Optimal Policies for Avoiding World War III." YouTube video, posted August 1, 2012. Accessed April 4, 2013. http://www.youtube.com/watch?v=sLcI3jBbi6Y.

————"House Prices: Expect the Worst." *MoneyWeek*. November 7, 2007. http://www.moneyweek.com/investments/property/house-prices-expect-the-worst.

————, ed. *The Losses of Nations: Deadweight Politics Versus Public Rent Dividends.* London: Othila Press, 1998.

————*The Power in the Land: An Inquiry into Unemployment, the Profits Crisis and Land Speculation.* London: Shepheard-Walwyn, 1983.

————The *Predator Culture: The Systemic Roots and Intent of Organised Violence.* London: Shepheard-Walwyn, 2010.

————*Ricardo's Law: House Prices and the Great Tax Clawback Scam.* London: Shepheard-Walwyn, 2006.

————*The Silver Bullet.* London: International Union for Land Value Taxation, 2008.

————*The Traumatised Society: How to Outlaw Cheating and Save Our Civilisation.* London: Shepheard-Walwyn, 2012.

Hartzok, Alanna. "The Wright Act, California, USA SWOT Analysis." Accessed September 12, 2014. http://www.earthrights.net/wg/swot-california.html.

Holland, Tim G., Garry D. Peterson, and Andrew Gonzalez. "A Cross-National Analysis of How Economic Inequality Predicts Biodiversity Loss." *Conservation Biology* 23, no. 5 (2009): 1304–13. http://onlinelibrary.wiley.com/doi/10.1111/j.1523-1739.2009.01207.x/full.

Hong, Yu-Hung. "Can Leasing Public Land Be an Alternative Source of Local Public Finance?" Working paper, Lincoln Institute of Land Policy, January 1996. http://www.lincolninst.edu/pubs/145_Can-Leasing-Public-Land-Be-An-Alternative-Source-of-Local-Public-Finance-.

"Hong Kong Land Lease Reform, Part 1." Webb-Site Reports. October 7, 2010. http://www.webb-site.com/articles/leases1.asp

Hoyt, Homer. *One Hundred Years of Land Values in Chicago: The Relationship of the Growth of Chicago to the Rise of Its Land Values, 1830–1933.* Washington, DC: Beard Books, 2000.

Hungerford, Thomas L. "Changes in Income Inequality Among U.S. Tax Filers between 1991 and 2006: The Role of Wages, Capital Income, and Taxes." Working paper, January 23, 2013. http://dx.doi.org/10.2139/ssrn.2207372.

Jomo, K. S. "Globalisation, Liberalisation, Poverty and Income Inequality in Southeast Asia." Working Paper No. 185, OECD Development Centre, 2001. http://www.oecd.org/dev/asia-pacific/34319665.pdf.

Jones, Frederic J., and Fred Harrison. *The Chaos Makers*. London: Othila Press, 1997.

Jones, Sophia. "Sweden Wants Your Trash." *The Two Way* (blog). National Public Radio, October 28, 2012. http://www.npr.org/blogs/thetwo-way/2012/10/28/163823839/sweden-wants-your-trash.

Kelly, Morgan. "Inequality and Crime." *Review of Economics and Statistics* 82, no 4 (November 2000): 530–39. http://www.jstor.org/discover/10.2307/2646649?uid=2&uid=4&sid=21101703919597.

Klooster, Daniel. "Institutional Choice, Community, and Struggle: A Case Study of Forest Co-Management in Mexico." *World Development* 28 (2000): 1–20.

Liou, Daniel He-chiun. "Poverty (and Social Exclusion) Measurement in Taiwan." Presentation given at the Second Peter Townsand Memorial Conference, January 23, 2011. Access October 26, 2012. http://www.slideserve.com/clove/poverty-and-social-exclusion-measurement-in-taiwan.

Love, John F. "Big Macs, Fries, and Real Estate." *Financial Executive* 3, no. 4 (April 1987): 20–26. http://connection.ebscohost.com/c/articles/14781568/big-macs-fries-real-estate.

Marx, Karl, and Friedrich Engels. *The Communist Manifesto*. Middlesex, England: Echo Library, 2009.

Mikkelson, Gregory M., Andrew Gonzalez, A., and Garry D. Peterson. "Economic Inequality Predicts Biodiversity Loss." PLoS ONE 2, no. 5 (2007). http://www.plosone.org/article/info%3Adoi%2F10.1371%2Fjournal.pone.0000444.

Mitra, Sáradá Charan. *The Land-Law of Bengal*. Calcutta: Thacker,

Spink & Co.: 1898. http://books.google.com/books?id=RAo-bAAAAYAAJ.

Moody, J. Scott, Wendy P. Warcholik, and Scott A. Hodge. *"The Rising Cost of Complying with the Federal Income Tax."* Tax Foundation Report 138, December 2005. http://taxfoundation.org/sites/taxfoundation.org/files/docs/sr138.pdf.

National Young Farmers Coalition. "Building a Future with Farmers: Challenges Faced by Young, American Farmers and a National Strategy to Help Them Succeed." November 2011. http://www.youngfarmers.org/reports/Building_A_Future_With_Farmers.pdf.

Nickerson, Cynthia, Robert Ebel, Allison Borchers, and Fernando Carriazo. "Major Uses of Land in the United States, 2007" U.S. Department of Agriculture Economic Research Service Bulletin 89, December 2011. http://www.ers.usda.gov/media/188404/eib89_2_.pdf.

Nickerson, Cynthia, Mitchell Morehart, Todd Kuethe, Jayson Beckman, Jennifer Ifft, and Ryan Williams. "Trends in U.S. Farmland Values and Ownership." U.S. Department of Agriculture *Economic Information Bulletin* 92, February 2012. http://www.ers.usda.gov/media/377487/eib92_2_.pdf.

Nock, Albert J. "Henry George: Unorthodox American." 1933. http://www.wealthandwant.com/docs/Nock_HGUA.htm.

Olmstead, Alan L., and Paul Rhode. "Average Acreage per Farm, by Region and State: 1850–1997." In *Historical Statistics of the United States, Earliest Times to the Present: Millennial Edition*, edited by Susan B. Carter, et al. New York: Cambridge University Press, 2006.

Ricardo, David. *On the Principles of Political Economy and Taxation*. 1817. http://www.econlib.org/library/Ricardo/ricP.html.

Rothbard, Murray N. "The Single Tax: Economic and Moral Implications and a Reply to Georgist Criticisms." In The Logic of Action One: Method, Money, and the Austrian School, 294–310. London: Edward Elgar, 1997. http://mises.org/rothbard/georgism.pdf.

Schenk, Catherine R. "Economic History of Hong Kong." EH.Net Encyclopedia, edited by Robert Whaples. March 16, 2008. http://eh.net/encyclopedia/economic-history-of-hong-kong.

Smith, Jeffery J. "Where a Tax Reform Has Worked: 28 Case Studies." The Progress Report. Last modified September 15, 2011. http://www.progress.org/tpr/36000.

"The Story of Crowfoot's Encounter." Blackfoot Crossing Historical Park. http://www.blackfootcrossing.ca/treaties.html.

Sullivan, Dan. "Property Tax Rates and Housing Affordability." Accessed September 12, 2014. http://savingcommunities.org/issues/taxes/property/affordabilitycharts.html.

Taxpayer Advocate Service. "The Time for Tax Reform Is Now." MSP #1, 2011. http://www.taxpayeradvocate.irs.gov/files/MSP1_Tax%20Reform.pdf.

The Times Herald. "Milton Friedman Interviewed." December 1, 1978. http://www.cooperativeindividualism.org/friedman-milton_interview-1978.html.

United Nations Conference on Trade and Development. "Trade and Environment Review 2013." http://unctad.org/en/Publications Library/ditcted2012d3_en.pdf.

U.S. Census Bureau. "Annual Estimates of the Population for the United States, Regions, States, and Puerto Rico: April 1, 2010 to July 1, 2013." 2013. http://www.census.gov/popest/data/state/totals/2013/tables/NST-EST2013-01.xls.

———"Historical Income Tables: Households." 2010. http://www.census.gov/hhes/www/income/data/historical/household.

———"Household Income for States: 2009 and 2010." 2011.

http://www.census.gov/prod/2011pubs/acsbr10-02.pdf.

———"Land and Water Area of States and Other Entities: 2008." 2012. http://www.census.gov/compendia/statab/2012/tables/12s0358.pdf.

U.S. Department of Agriculture. "Summary Report: 2007 National Resources Inventory." Natural Resources Conservation Service, Washington, DC, and Center for Survey Statistics and Methodology, Iowa State University, Ames, Iowa, 2009. http://www.nrcs.usda.gov/Internet/FSE_DOCUMENTS/stelprdb1041379.pdf.

———"Providing Resources for Beginning Farmers and Ranchers." USDA blog. May 8, 2009. http://blogs.usda.gov/2009/05/08/providing-resources-for-beginning-farmers-and-ranchers/.

Wenzlick, Roy. "The Coming Boom in Real Estate." *Reader's Digest* 29, no. 171, July 1936.

WNYC. "Joseph Stiglitz Explains the Price of Inequality." *The Leonard Lopate Show.* June 6, 2012. http://www.wnyc.org/shows/lopate/2012/jun/06/joseph-stiglitz-explains-price-inequality.

World Wildlife Fund. "Living Planet Report 2012: Biodiversity, Biocapacity, and Better Choices." http://www.footprintnetwork.org/images/uploads/LPR_2012.pdf.

Yglesias, Matthew. "What's All the Land in America Worth?" *Slate*, December 20, 2013. http://www.slate.com/blogs/moneybox/2013/12/20/value_of_all_land_in_the_united_states.html.

ENDNOTES

1. The term *wealth production* means the process by which more wealth is created, and this includes not just making a product, but also its transportation and distribution. A computer at a nearby store is more valuable than a computer located at a distant factory where it can't yet be used.

2. The term *land* doesn't include raw materials; since raw materials have been processed, they're considered capital. For example, oil reserves still in the ground are allocated to land, while oil extracted from the ground is capital.

3. A person can also make an income by assisting others in their contributions to society, such as by investing in productive enterprises. A person who helps others contribute to society by definition also contributes to society.

4. Classical economists have also used the term *interest* to describe the return on capital goods. However, the term *interest* can too easily be confused with our contemporary understanding of the word *interest*, which purely refers to the cost of borrowing money and has little to do with the return on capital goods.

5. The economic definition of *rent* is different from our conversational use of the word *rent*: When tenants pay rent to landlords, landlords only receive economic rent on the land upon which their home is located since this income on land is unearned and not the result of wealth production; meanwhile, since buildings are capital goods, the part of the income that pays for the house is a capital return. When a person buys a home, the purchase price consists of both a rent portion for the land (a one-time capitalization of all the future rent the buyer expects to receive from this particular piece of land) and a capital return portion for the

building (a one-time capitalization of all the future capital returns the buyer expects to receive from the building). The technically inclined reader who has had some previous exposure to economics will most likely be familiar with the neoclassical definition of *economic rent*, which refers to all income above and beyond the income that's necessary to put a factor into production. Classical economists have traditionally used the term *rent* to refer to incomes from land. The classical definition of *land rent* is a subset of the neoclassical definition of *economic rent* because more money doesn't produce more land, and therefore all money that's used to put land into production is also economic rent. In this discussion, we'll focus on the classical definition of rent from land, because it's a significant way by which individuals extract unearned wealth from society.

6. David Ricardo, *On the Principles of Political Economy and Taxation* (1817), chap. 2. The *Law of Rent* was first popularized in 1817 by economist David Ricardo (1772–1823) through his work *On the Principles of Political Economy and Taxation*, an informative work that illuminates the mechanism by which land obtains its value. Although Ricardo focused on "the powers of the soil" as he described the added benefits that one land has over another, he laid the groundwork for a deeper understanding of the role that land plays in society. Ricardo's Law of Rent was later enhanced by the work of Johann von Thünen (1783–1850), who developed the first serious treatment of spatial economics. He called land rent *locational rent* since a land's value is dependent upon its location relative to the people, goods, and services that exist in the surrounding environment.

7. Charles Duhigg and Keith Bradsher, "How the U.S. Lost Out on iPhone Work," New York Times, January 21, 2012. A poignant example that illustrates the critical importance of location was highlighted in a *New York Times* article on January 21, 2012,

which described why Apple Inc., the maker of sleek consumable electronics, decided to relocate its factories from the United States to China in 2005. Contrary to common belief, the cost of labor was not the driving force behind Apple's decision. According to the article:

For Mr. Cook [Apple's CEO], the focus on Asia "came down to two things," said one former high-ranking Apple executive. Factories in Asia "can scale up and down faster" and "Asian supply chains have surpassed what's in the U.S." The result is that "we can't compete at this point," the executive said.

"The entire supply chain is in China now," said another former high-ranking Apple executive. "You need a thousand rubber gaskets? That's the factory next door. You need a million screws? That factory is a block away. You need that screw made a little bit different? It will take three hours."

Thus, even if Apple had negotiated lower wages with its employees, production would still have been expensive because Apple's suppliers no longer offered Apple the same speed and convenience of operating near Apple's assembly lines in the United States. While many factors have led to the loss of America's manufacturing base, the astronomical cost of land—a direct byproduct of the monopolization of land—should be counted as one of the most significant contributors. Location remains a critical aspect in today's economy, yet companies' balance sheets generally don't account for the financial benefits that companies receive from existing in certain locations.

8. Monopolies occur whenever supply either can't or won't be increased despite heightened demand: In other words, whenever there aren't enough goods and services to go around. This creates a scarcity that makes goods and services cost more than they would if all participants had the ability to produce as many goods and services as the market required. This higher cost increases the

incomes for monopolists, and this additional revenue exceeds the free market value of the goods and services that were provided.

9. This process is also known as *imputed rent.* In our example, the property owner has an opportunity cost of $6,000, income the property owner forgoes if she chooses to use the land herself, which is why to her the land still has a cost. But because the property owner claims this land value for herself, she receives benefits worth $6,000, and therefore her bottom line remains $8,000.

10. An illustration might be helpful in order to facilitate further understanding. Capitalism allows individuals to receive incomes from wages (W), capital returns (C), and rent (R), and then partially taxes this income for society. Socialism taxes this income to a greater extent. Communism seizes most incomes from wages, capital returns, and rent. A sustainable economy, however, won't allow individuals to take the rents created by communities, but does allow them to keep all that they produce.

ILLUSTRATION 3-2: CAPITALISM, SOCIALISM, AND COMMUNISM VERSUS A SUSTAINABLE ECONOMIC MODEL

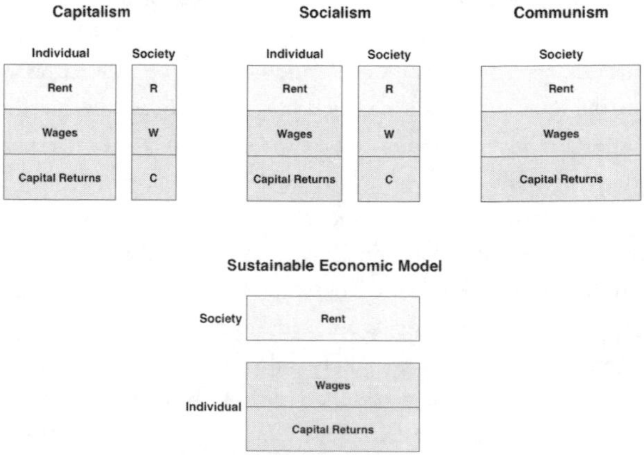

ENDNOTES

11. Mason Gaffney and Fred Harrison, *The Corruption of Economics* (London: Shepheard-Walwyn, 2007), 29. Toward the end of the nineteenth century, the philosopher and economist Henry George was gaining unprecedented public support for his land-reform proposals in the United States, Great Britain, and elsewhere, and was even close to implementing them. Henry George's success and popular support, according to Gaffney, "became a clear and present political danger, and challenge to the landed and intellectual establishments of the world." Gaffney claims that "few people realize to what a degree the founders of Neoclassical economics changed the discipline for the express purpose of deflecting George, discomfiting his followers, and frustrating future students seeking to follow his arguments."

   During that time, economists such as John B. Clark and Frank A. Fetter began promoting an economic theory that didn't recognize the difference between land and capital; due to their influence, Clark and Fetter were able to persuade other economists to abandon the critical distinction between land and capital.

   Karl Marx, too, failed to differentiate between land and capital, and by doing so unwittingly played into the hands of rent seekers who had little interest in making it known that land—not capital—was chiefly what enabled people to extract unearned gains from society. Even though Marx failed to make that critical distinction, he did recognize that the rent of land needed to be collected for public purposes. He didn't, however, distinguish the rent of land (a public good) from the private use of land, and called for the collectivization of land altogether in the first plank of *The Communist Manifesto*.

12. Farmland, which tends to be of insignificant value compared to urban land, is sometimes an exception.

13. In some cases, improvements that have a significant impact on their environment—Disneyland, major airports, etc.—can indi-

rectly influence the value of the land upon which they exist by influencing the desirability of the surrounding land, but those are the exception rather than the rule.

14. This statement can be expressed concisely with the following two equations:

Wealth produced by labor and capital using nature's gifts = total wealth produced.

Total wealth produced minus wealth extracted from society (*rent*) = wealth left over to pay for goods and services.

15. As we can see in the figure below, growth in land values (indicated by the top graph, which shows growth of residential land values in the United States) tends to outpace growth in wages and capital returns (approximated by the remaining graphs, which show growth of household incomes for the lowest through highest fifth of households in the United States by income). Higher-earning households are presumably more likely to profit from land, because they're more likely to own property.

ILLUSTRATION 4-1: LAND VALUES VERSUS WAGES

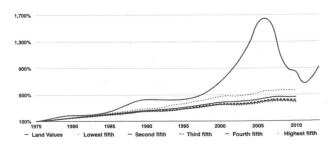

Land Value data: Morris A. Davis and Jonathan Heathcote, "The Price and Quantity of Residential Land in the United States," *Journal of Monetary Economics* 54, no. 8 (2007): 2595–620.

Household Income data: U.S. Census Bureau, 2010.

16. John F. Love, "Big Macs, Fries, and Real Estate." *Financial Executive*, 4 (April 1987), 20–26. The success of McDonald's, for example, can largely be attributed to its real-estate policy.

17. According to a study of tax filings in the United States from 1991 to 2006, incomes from dividends and capital gains—which contain land-value gains—were the greatest contributors to the wealth divide in the United States during that time:

ILLUSTRATION 4-2: CHANGES IN INCOME INEQUALITY AMONG U.S. TAX FILERS BETWEEN 1991 AND 2006: THE ROLE OF WAGES, CAPITAL INCOME, AND TAXES

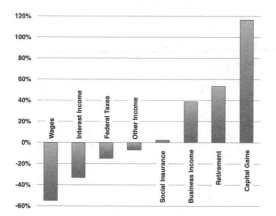

Thomas Hungerford, "Changes in Income Inequality Among U.S. Tax Filers between 1991 and 2006: The Role of Wages, Capital Income, and Taxes" (working paper, January 23, 2013).

By allowing property owners to profit from land, we systematically reward them with financial resources that never were, in truth, theirs to begin with. The entire boom in housing prices in the early 2000s was essentially a grand theft as housing prices increased without corresponding increases in real wealth. Even today, with an ongoing slump in housing prices in many parts of the world, we see savvy real-estate investors buying up inexpensive properties because they know that, in time, property prices will rise again, giving them the renewed ability to profit from future land-value gains.

18. Using 2010 data provided by the U.S. Census of the *Gini coefficient* of wealth inequality for each U.S. state and Washington D.C., we see that, indeed, we have greater wealth inequality in places with a higher population density. The *Gini coefficient* is a mathematical indicator, used in this case to highlight disparities in the distribution of wealth. A Gini coefficient of 0 indicates *perfect* wealth equality, where every family or household has the same income (meaning wealth is most evenly distributed throughout society), while a Gini coefficient of 1.0 indicates a situation where one family or household has all the income (meaning wealth is most unequally distributed throughout society). A Gini coefficient anywhere from 0.419 (for the state of Utah) to 0.532 (for Washington, D.C.) is a comparatively high coefficient for any developed nation.

ILLUSTRATION 4-3: POPULATION DENSITY BY GINI COEFFICIENT FOR EACH U.S. STATE AND D.C.

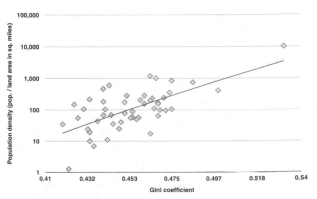

◇ Population density by Gini coefficient for each U.S. State and Washington D.C.

Population: U.S. Census Bureau, "Annual Estimates of the Population for the United States, Regions, States, and Puerto Rico: April 1, 2010 to July 1, 2011."

Area: U.S. Census Bureau, "Land and Water Area of States and Other Entities: 2008," 2012.

Gini coefficient: U.S. Census Bureau, "Household Income for States: 2009 and 2010," 2011.

In places and cultures where private parties aren't able to profit as much from land at the expense of other people, wealth inequality has a lower correlation to population density. Taiwan, for example, is a small yet financially prosperous island with a fairly large population; it underwent substantial land reforms in the 1940s (K. S. Jomo, "Globalisation, Liberalisation, Poverty and Income Inequality in Southeast Asia," OECD Development Centre, 2001). In 2009, Taiwan's population density of 1,658 people per square mile was greater than that of any U.S. state, and yet its Gini coefficient was only 0.35 (Daniel He-chiun. Liou, "Poverty and Social Exclusion Measurement in Taiwan," 2011). Taiwan's Gini coefficient was even lower in the 1980s, before the government changed its land policies to allow more land values to be claimed by private land speculators.

19. Morgan Kelly, "Inequality and Crime," *The Review of Economics and Statistics* 82, no. 4 (November 2000): 530–39.

20. Fred Harrison, *The Power in the Land* (London: Shepheard-Walwyn, 1983).

21. Fred Harrison, "House Prices: Expect the Worst," *MoneyWeek*, November 7, 2007. Several economists and statisticians before Harrison also discovered this real-estate cycle: One of the first was real-estate appraiser Homer Hoyt, who described the cycle in 1933 in his published PhD dissertation, *One Hundred Years of Land Values in Chicago: The Relationship of the Growth of Chicago to the Rise of Its Land Values, 1830–1933* (Washington, DC: Beard Books, 2000).

Another was real-estate appraiser Roy Wenzlick, who made accurate predictions about the real-estate market through his article "The Coming Boom in Real Estate," first published in 1936 and reprinted that same year in *Reader's Digest* 29, no. 171 (July 1936).

22. Using historical land-value data from the Lincoln Institute of Land Policy, we can create a graph of land-value changes in the United States for the last thirty-five years, which allows us to see how this theory plays out in practice. Diminished growth in land values has always been followed by several months, if not years, of economic depression (shaded gray areas). Here, we see that every depression was preceded by declines in the growth of land values (main graph, declines indicated by black descending line). The economic pullback of 2001, which was brought on in part by the run-up of the tech bubble and the events of September 11, 2001, is not indicated here since it can properly be characterized as a minor recession rather than a depression.

ILLUSTRATION 5-2: LAND VALUES AND ECONOMIC DEPRESSIONS

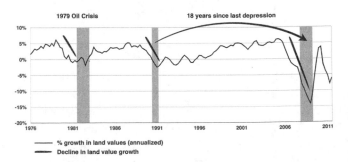

Morris A. Davis and Jonathan Heathcote, "The Price and Quantity of Residential Land in the United States," *Journal of Monetary Economics* 54, no. 8 (2007): 2595–620.

ENDNOTES

23. Frederic J. Jones and Fred Harrison, *The Chaos Makers* (London: Othila Press, 1997).

24. Fred Foldvary, "The Business Cycle: A Geo-Austrian Synthesis," *American Journal of Economics and Sociology* 56, no 4 (1997): 521–41. Foldvary called the theory of these eighteen-year cycles the *Geo-Austrian cycle theory*, in reference to influences from both the so-called Georgist and the Austrian school of economics. The Austrian school claims that an excessive expansion of the money supply by a central monetary authority such as by the Federal Reserve Bank of the United States artificially lowers the interest rate, which thereby encourages unreasonable investments into, among other things, real estate. Since this behavior eventually encourages a series of bad investments, interest rates soon begin to rise, and this leads to higher borrowing costs, a restriction in the money supply, and subsequently to an economic depression. Other economists such as Mason Gaffney have also synthesized major aspects from both the Geoist and Austrian schools into a unified theory (see Mason Gaffney, "Causes of Downturns: An Austro-Georgist Synthesis," working paper, 1982).

In his numerous scholarly and popular articles on the synthesis of the Austrian monetary school and the land perspective as it relates to the U.S. real-estate market and economy, Foldvary documents real-estate cycles in the United States: While there have been some significant variations in the cycle, the average time for each cycle remains about eighteen years. An interesting side note is that the Great Depression that began in 1929 took place shortly after land values hit a peak and then contracted. It is often blamed on a restriction of the supply of money initiated by the Federal Reserve; few are aware that it might have been primarily caused by land speculation.

TABLE 5-3: PEAKS IN LAND VALUES, PEAKS IN CONSTRUCTION, AND ECONOMIC DEPRESSIONS

Peaks in Land Values	Interval (years)	Peaks in Construction	Interval (years)	Economic Depressions	Interval (years)
1818	—	—	—	1819	—
1836	18	1836	—	1837	18
1854	18	1856	20	1857	20
1872	18	1871	15	1873	16
1890	18	1892	21	1893	20
1907	17	1909	17	1918	25
1925	18	1925	16	1929	11
World War II					
First Oil Crisis					
1973	—	1972	—	1973	—
Second Oil Crisis					
1979	16	1978	14	1980	17
1989		1986		1990	
2006	17	2006	20	2008	18
Averages:	17.50		15.38		18.13

25. Fred Foldvary, "The Depression of 2026," *The Progress Report*, March 19, 2012.

26. "The Story of Crowfoot's Encounter," Blackfoot Crossing Historical Park, n.d.

27. Anthony D. Barnosky et al. "Approaching a State Shift in Earth's Biosphere," *Nature* 486 (June 2012): 52–58. I would like to mention an interesting study led by biologist Anthony Barnosky, published in 2012 in the journal *Nature*. The authors of this study, twenty-two respected scientists from fields including zoology, paleontology, and ecology, note that local ecosystems generally undergo significant shifts once their decline crosses a certain threshold, which empirical data demonstrates to be anywhere from 50 to 90 percent of their original size. The authors propose that our global ecosystem might behave similarly. According to the study, humanity has already encroached upon 43 percent of the Earth's ecosystem, as measured by our use of total habitable land; the authors conservatively estimate that we will hit

the 50 percent mark no later than 2025.
http://unitism.co/stateshift

ILLUSTRATION 6-1: ECOCIDE

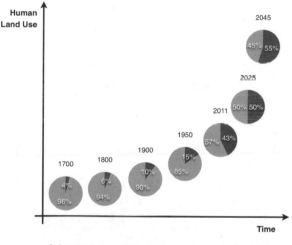

28. Robert V. Andelson, *Commons without Tragedy: Protecting the Environment from Overpopulation—A New Approach.* (London: Shepheard-Walwyn, 1991). Robert Andelson, editor of *A Commons without Tragedy: Protecting the Environment from Overpopulation—A New Approach*, says it well: "It is incontrovertible, I think, that the rapidly-increasing destruction of the Amazon rainforest is directly attributable to the fact that the Amazon basin is the only part of Brazil where free or cheap land is available, and this, in turn, is attributable to the fact that nearly four-fifths of Brazil's arable acreage is covered by sprawling latifundia, half of which are held by speculators who produce nothing. Were the artificial

scarcity of available land in the rest of Brazil corrected, pressure on the Amazon basin would obviously cease."

29. Even the word *environment* points to this disconnection: It stems from the Old French *environer*, "to surround, enclose, encircle," implying a subject that is separate from the objects it's surrounded by.

30. Jesus also spoke a telling parable (Mark 12):

A man planted a vineyard. He put a wall around it, dug a pit for the winepress and built a watchtower. Then he rented the vineyard to some farmers and moved to another place. 2 At harvest time he sent a servant to the tenants to collect from them some of the fruit of the vineyard. 3 But they seized him, beat him and sent him away empty-handed. 4 Then he sent another servant to them; they struck this man on the head and treated him shamefully. 5 He sent still another, and that one they killed. He sent many others; some of them they beat, others they killed. 6 "He had one left to send, a son, whom he loved. He sent him last of all, saying, 'They will respect my son.' 7 "But the tenants said to one another, 'This is the heir. Come, let's kill him, and the inheritance will be ours.' 8 So they took him and killed him, and threw him out of the vineyard. 9 "What then will the owner of the vineyard do? He will come and kill those tenants and give the vineyard to others.

While parables can be read in many ways, one possible interpretation is that the *vineyard owner* represents the totality of life (or God), the *vineyard* the Earth, and the *son* our sacred relationship to life or God. If human beings view themselves as owners over that which they only rent (the Earth), and if they eliminate their sacred relationship to that which gives life in an attempt to attain ownership over the Earth, life itself will eventually bring about the extinction of humankind.

31. Sáradá Charan Mitra, *The Land-Law of Bengal*, 1898.

32. Charles Eisenstein, author of *The More Beautiful World Our Hearts Know Is Possible*, summarizes this perspective beautifully in his book *The Ascent of Humanity*:

America was not stolen from the Indians, because the Indians never owned it. The land was not property. While pre-agricultural peoples often have a tribal territory, they would be appalled at the idea that land could be owned. Is not the Earth a being greater than any human, or even any group of humans? How can a greater *belong* to a lesser? To presume to own a piece of the Earth, to say it is *mine*, is from the indigenous perspective a sacrilege so audacious as to be unthinkable. To reduce the Earth to property and eventually to money is indeed to make a greater into a lesser, to turn the sacred into the profane, the divine into the human, the infinite into the quantified. I can think of no better definition of sacrilege than that.

33. Article 3 of the United Nations Universal Declaration of Human Rights states that: "Article 3. Everyone has the right to life, liberty, and security of person." The right to land—or at least the right to the value of land—is missing: Article 3. Everyone has the right to life, liberty, land, and security of person.

Article 17, too, doesn't have the property rights enshrined. Currently, it reads as follows:

"Article 17. (1) Everyone has the right to own property alone as well as in association with others. (2) No one shall be arbitrarily deprived of his property."

A third option, which includes the right to the benefits provided by nature, ought to be added to Article 17 so that it reads as follows:

Article 17. (1) Everyone has the right to own property alone as well as in association with others. (2) No one shall be arbitrarily deprived of his or her property. (3) Everyone has a right to an equal share in the gifts of nature. The gifts of nature shall be equally shared among all.

34. Murray N. Rothbard, "The Single Tax: Economic and Moral Implications and a Reply to Georgist Criticisms," in The Logic of

Action One: Method, Money, and the Austrian School (London: Edward Elgar, 1997) 294–310. In this paper, Rothbard explicitly took aim at the ideas of the nineteenth-century economic philosopher Henry George, who argued that land values ought to be taxed. There are several other points in Rothbard's paper that point to a profound misunderstanding of Henry George's teachings and baffle rational thought; in another case, he confused taxes on the value of unimproved land with a property tax on the value of improvements to land. An even-minded rebuttal of Rothbard's arguments can be found by Gene DeNardo's "A Critique of Murray Rothbard's Critique of the Georgist Argument" (2009).

35. Henry George, *Progress and Poverty: An Inquiry into the Cause of Industrial Depressions and of Increase of Want with Increase of Wealth: The Remedy*, Book VIII, chap. 2, para. 12, 1879. The economic philosopher Henry George expressed it quite succinctly: "Let the individuals who now hold land still retain possession of what they are pleased to call 'their' land. Let them buy and sell, and bequeath and devise it. We may safely leave them the shell, if we take the kernel. It is not necessary to confiscate land; it is only necessary to confiscate rent."

36. Illustration 8-1: Community Land Contributions and Land Prices

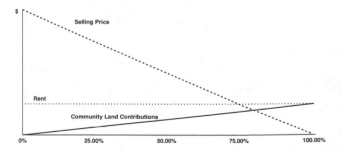

Community land contributions as % of total rental value

The above graph is a theoretical illustration that shows us how community land contributions and rental values are connected. Because land users have to reimburse their communities for their use of land, land selling prices (signified by the dashed line *Selling Price*) drop from their monopolized price; selling prices further decrease the more community land contributions (signified by the solid line *Community Land Contributions*) approach the rental value of land (signified by the dotted line *Rent*).

Community land contributions tend to decrease the selling price of land in relationship to its rental value; its actual rental value remains unchanged, at least over the short term. However, the efficiencies gained from community land contributions can create so much wealth in any given area (and thus increase the rental value of land) that land prices can even increase, but still decrease in relationship to the rental value of land and to the total amount of new wealth that has been created. Especially once corporate, income, and sales taxes are removed, people's paying capacity for central locations will actually increase, and this can boost land values in well-serviced neighborhoods overall.

Since the size of community land contributions is a fraction of the land's rental value, the absolute size of the payment will always approximate the rental value of land; if community land contributions were greater than the rental value of land, people wouldn't use that land (in fact, you'd have to pay them an incentive to use that land), which is why community land contributions are always less than the rental value of land. Therefore, since community land contributions lower the selling price of land and simultaneously increase its holding cost—up to but never greater than its rental value—we see from this graph that community land contributions help us move from a monopoly model on land toward a rental model in such a way that the private use of land can be retained. Since the rental price of land on the open market is never greater than what people are willing to pay in order to generate a profit from their productive use of land, community land contributions will always be lower than the amount at which an entity that puts land to good use can still turn a profit, which is why the community land contribution model represents a smart approach to land use, both from a societal as from an individual perspective.

37. Until 1997, at which point it reverted back to Chinese rule.

38. Hong Kong Land Lease Reform, Part I (October 7, 2010).

39. According to one study, the British colonial government was able to recapture, through its leasehold arrangements, about 39 percent of all the land-value increases that occurred during the period from 1970 to 1991 (Yu-Hung Hong, "Can Leasing Public Land Be an Alternative Source of Local Public Finance?" working paper, Lincoln Institute of Land Policy, 1996). In addition to leasing out land, the government of Hong Kong also levied taxes on residential and commercial rental income, which, together with its land-leasing program, allowed the government to recoup, on average, *up to 79 percent of its infrastructure investments.* These revenues also allowed the government to heavily invest in ambitious public-housing programs and provide free public education for children up to the age of fifteen (Catherine Schenk, "Economic History of Hong Kong," *EH.Net Encyclopedia*, edited by Robert Whaples, March 16, 2008).

40. I was born and grew up in Hong Kong and saw firsthand opulent wealth existing next to immense poverty. Hong Kong is a flawed example, I admit, but nonetheless one that stands out. Interestingly enough, these early childhood impressions stirred in me a desire to help remedy wealth inequality and economic inequity.

41. Alaskan voters approved a constitutional amendment in 1976, which mandated that at least 25 percent of all mineral lease rentals, royalties, royalty sales proceeds, federal mineral revenue-

sharing payments and bonuses received by the state are placed in a permanent fund called the *Alaska Permanent Fund*. In 2013 each resident of Alaska received $900.

42. In the case of both Alaska and Norway, however, public revenues only include revenues from oil and no significant revenues from land.

43. These reform policies were inspired by one of China's spiritual leaders, Sun Yat-sen. Sun Yat-sen, in turn, was directly influenced by the ideas of the nineteenth-century economic philosopher Henry George.

44. For an excellent overview, see Alanna Hartzok, "The Wright Act, California, USA SWOT Analysis," n.d.

45. When a person buys land, the property's purchase price reflects a one-time capitalization of all the future benefits the new property owner expects to receive from the newly acquired property. The purchase price also reflects any expected charges that are to be levied against the property in the future. If a community were to unexpectedly charge the new property owner for ownership of land, the new property owner would have to pay for land a second time because the initial purchase price didn't reflect those charges. And since community land contributions decrease property values, property owners would be unable to recuperate a significant portion of the money they paid to acquire their properties.

46. While a compensation plan would be a costly endeavor, it would help prevent the economic booms and busts that are driven by the eighteen-year real-estate cycle. According to Foldvary, a compensation plan would allow the economy to be "so much more productive that an ever-increasing income from land would enable the government to reduce its borrowing and eventually buy back the bonds."

   It also makes political and practical sense to ensure that property owners won't lose out financially in the short run by transitioning to an economy based on community land contributions. For this, we have anecdotal evidence: When General Chiang Kai-shek retreated to Taiwan after losing the civil war in mainland China, General Chiang decided to reform the economy of Taiwan, which at that time was mired in poverty and overpopulation: The majority of people were landless, hunger-afflicted peasants, while fewer than twenty families monopolized the land of the entire island (Jeffery J. Smith, *"Where a Tax Reform Has Worked,"* September 15, 2011). When Taiwan enacted land reform and began collecting land contributions, it compensated these landowners with bonds (Fred Foldvary, "The Pre-existing Land Value Problem," *The Progress Report*, April 8, 2013). Everyone ended up benefitting from a smooth transition toward a more just and efficient economy.

47. In his work "The Ultimate Tax Reform: Public Revenue from Land Rent," Foldvary recommends ten steps for such a transition (the term *land rent* can be used interchangeably with *land contributions*):

1. Each county expands its register of all real estate and the title holders to include all lands owned by governments and previously non-registered entities.

2. Local real estate taxes are split into two taxes, one on land value and one on improvements.

3. The county real estate assessment function is transferred to land value assessment boards, comprised of representatives from the federal, state, county, and municipal governments as well as real estate professionals and scholars. These boards appoint assessors and establish an appeals process, similar to current real estate tax appeals.

4. All land is assessed at its current market value.

5. Over a period of years, depending on how much land values already have fallen in anticipation of the shift to land rent collection, the tax on improvements is reduced, while land rent collections are increased. (An immediate shift to land rent, with other taxes reduced or abolished, could be compensated, for those with net losses, with special bonds whose face-value interest payments would decrease over time; this would have an effect similar to the gradual increase in land rent.)

6. *Sales taxes, tariffs, and excise taxes are reduced and eventually eliminated.*

7. *The personal exemption in federal income taxes is raised each year, until it eventually includes all income, at which time all state and federal personal income taxes are abolished. The taxation of corporate profits is also phased out.*

8. *The rent of material land (minerals, oil, water, etc.), from the electromagnetic spectrum, from naturally growing forests, and from other elements of nature is collected at gradually increasing rates up to a substantial amount, if not all, of the unimproved rental value.*

9. *An amendment to the Constitution is enacted prohibiting any taxation of wages, sales, profits, value-added, or produced wealth and establishing the collection of land rent and other nature rents, along with voluntary user fees and charges for pollution and congestion, as the only sources of public revenues. The amendment also establishes a land rent commission with representatives from the federal, state, local, territorial, and indigenous-nation governments to divide the rents raised. Generally, rents raised from offshore oil and water, atmospheric pollution, airline routes, and other continental uses would be allocated to the federal government, and the rest would be allocated to the state, local, territorial, and indigenous-nation governments. If the national government needs additional revenue, it is obtained from the state or territorial governments in proportion to their land value, as was specified in the Articles of Confederation that preceded the U.S. Constitution.*

10. *Top-down revenue sharing from federal to state and from state to local government stops. Many services, functions, and agencies are transferred from the central government to the state/provincial and local governments.*

48. Adrian Wrigley called his concept *Location Value Covenants* (LVCs). In the interest of making the material more accessible to the reader, I've simplified the term to *land-use rights*. For more information on LVCs, visit the Systemic Fiscal Reform Group's website at http://systemicfiscalreform.org.

49. Without proper legislation regulating land-use rights, a community land trust may be required to hold title to the land. It then sells a tradable land-use right to the new land user. This permit also extends to all subsequent land users, provided that they make ongoing land contributions to the community land trust.

50. Land-use rights can also be applied to existing homeowners who don't wish to be tied to a mortgage.

51. An exception is taxes on wasteful consumption, which help to preserve the environment, not taxes on consumption in general. Food, for example, is a consumable we most certainly do not wish to tax, while we're wise to tax pollution.

52. "Idle Land, Unemployed Workers Caused by Incorrect Taxation," http://unitism.co/taxrevenues.

This graph uses the term *land value tax* in lieu of *community land contributions*; while these terms have different meanings, they have similar implications. The colored areas of this interactive graph (see link above) represent the total wealth created throughout our present economy. Our current taxes on wages, sales, and capital gains collect only a relatively small portion of the total wealth (red area), and the more wealth these taxes try to collect, the more they disrupt the economy. Because our present tax system takes rent out of the economy highly inefficiently, our system allows private parties to profit from land through seizing rent (green area), but at the same time also reduces the overall amount of wealth that could otherwise be had for the entire economy if less productive land were available to the economy (gray area). It's simply more profitable for property owners and associated financial institutions in our present tax system to withhold land from use and to then sell it at some other time for a profit. We can see in this interactive graph that our current tax system actually perpetuates wasteful use of land, while simultaneously encouraging a small portion of our total population to reap vast profits through private land speculation (green area). Furthermore, tax revenues on wages, sales, and capital gains are relatively meager (red area) compared to the public revenues that could be had from land contributions (orange area).

In addition to showing us some of the general principles of land contributions, this interactive graph also allows us to look at how some economic scenarios play out in theory:

The Law of Rent: Set all taxes to a minimum, set population to low, then gradually increase population—observe rents rise and wages fall.

The destructive effect of taxes on wages and capital gains: Gradually increase taxes on wages—observe unemployment and disused buildings increase.

The fallacy of Malthusian ideas: Set community land contributions to a maximum and taxes on wages to a minimum, then gradually increase population—observe revenue for public services increase.

The false appearance of the truth of Malthusian ideas under the current tax system: Set community land contributions to a minimum, set some taxes on wages, and gradually increase population—observe either wages or public revenues decrease.

The futility of taxing land and labor together: Set community land contributions to a maximum, set taxes on wages to a minimum, set population to be so high that the margin of production is below subsistence level, and gradually increase taxes on wages— observe revenue for public services decrease.

The applicability of the Laffer curve to taxes on wages: Set all taxes to a minimum, then gradually increase taxes on wages—observe public revenues increase at first, then decrease. (The Laffer curve is a representation of how most tax rates correlate to government revenue: The graph starts with a 0 percent tax rate and no government revenue, then rises to a maximum level of government revenue at an intermediate tax rate, and then falls again to zero revenue at a 100 percent tax rate.)

The nonapplicability of the Laffer curve to community land contributions: Set all taxes to a minimum, then gradually increase community land contributions—observe public revenues increase.

The potential usefulness of minimum wage laws in the absence of community land contributions: Set population to high, set some taxes on wages, set community land contributions to a minimum, set the minimum wage to low, and gradually increase the minimum wage—observe that a small increase in the minimum wage can raise the wages of a majority of the population with a relatively small cost in terms of unemployment, with landowners bearing most of the expense.

The uselessness of minimum wage laws in the presence of community land contributions: Set population to high, set taxes on wages to a minimum, set community land contributions to a maximum, set the minimum wage to low, and gradually increase the minimum wage—observe that any increase in the minimum wage comes at the expense of public revenues.

Interactive graph and overview courtesy of Daniel Syddall.

53. Based on a forty-hour work week per employee and 2,080 hours per year.
54. Taxpayer Advocate Service, "The Time for Tax Reform Is Now" *MSP* no. 1 (2011).
55. J. Scott Moody et al., "The Rising Cost of Complying with the Federal Income Tax," Tax Foundation Report 138, 2005.
56. Fred Harrison, Ricardo's Law: House Prices and the Great Tax Clawback Scam (London: Shepheard-Walwyn, 2006).

ENDNOTES

57. Cynthia Nickerson et al.,"Major Uses of Land in the United States, 2007" U.S. Department of Agriculture Economic Research Service Bulletin 89, December 2011.

58. Mason Gaffney, "$5.3 Trillion Rent of the USA," YouTube video interview, published November 14, 2013, accessed March 15, 2014.

59. The classical economists of old also realized the importance of keeping local communities empowered: The nineteenth-century economic philosopher Henry George, for example, realized that land contributions would automatically decentralize the government as much as possible. He was clear, however, to distinguish the *collection of land contributions*, which would empower local communities, from the *collectivization of land*: "The collectivist proposal to confiscate and manage natural resources as a state enterprise would have precisely the opposite effect—it would tend to make the state everything and the individual nothing" (Albert J. Nock, *Henry George: An Unorthodox American*, 1933).

60. The documentary "Real Estate 4 Ransom" poses a rhetorical question that drives this point home: "If you had all the money in the world, and I owned all the land, what would I charge you for your first night's rent?"

   But let the facts speak for themselves: For most of its existence, the U.S. economy operated on sound money prior to the establishment of the Federal Reserve in 1913, yet in settled parts of America people nonetheless experienced extreme wealth inequality as well as economic booms and busts. Not so in frontier towns, however, where land could still be had for very little: Wages there tended to be comparatively high, opportunities for employment were great, and economic booms and busts did not exist.

61. Economists throughout history have clearly stated that land contributions will not raise the rents of tenants but will eat into the profits of landowners, who do little work for the income they

receive. Adam Smith recognized this back in 1776 in his work *An Inquiry into the Nature and Causes of the Wealth of Nations*:

A tax upon ground-rents would not raise the rents of houses. It would fall altogether upon the owner of the ground-rent, who acts always as a monopolist, and exacts the greatest rent which can be got for the use of his ground. . . . Whether the tax was to be advanced by the inhabitant, or by the owner of the ground, would be of little importance. The more the inhabitant was obliged to pay for the tax, the less he would incline to pay for the ground; so that the final payment of the tax would fall altogether upon the owner of the ground-rent.

62. Assuming a property tax rate of 1 percent, $150,000 is the *privatized* location value of the property, claimed by the property owner. If the community collects a property tax of 1 percent on this property, and assuming an interest rate of 3 percent, the property's *untaxed* location value is $200,000, $50,000 of which is collected by the community.

The following calculation is for the interested reader (see the Appendix, The Math behind the Science, for more details). We can determine the property's pure location value with no property taxes using the following mathematical formula: P_{tax} equals the property's privatized location value of $150,000, which already factors in a property tax, P is the property's location value without a property tax, i is the current interest rate (in this case 3 percent), and t is the current property tax rate (in this case 1 percent).

$$P = P_{tax} \times \frac{i + t}{i} = \$150,000 \times \frac{4\%}{3\%} = \$200,000$$

63. If a community land trust is involved instead of a municipality, the community land trust holds title to the property and then sells to Susan an exclusive and transferable land use right (for more information, see Endnote 49). Thus, the community land

trust either pays $250,000 to the previous owner or receives the property as a donation from the previous owner, then sells to Susan an exclusive land use right for $130,000. Susan could either pay $130,000 in full or make a down payment of $50,000 to the community land trust and repay the remainder to the community land trust over time.

64. This new price makes sense, since Susan herself only paid $130,000 for the property. While Susan could immediately resell the property for $140,000 and make a profit of $10,000 through arbitrage after paying off her mortgage, her take-home profit will be negligible after closing costs and time and energy spent. The reason her new property sells for $140,000 and not $100,000 (which is the original sales price of $250,000 minus its location value of $150,000) is because the new property price contains the building value of $100,000 as well as a privatized—but significantly reduced—location value of $40,000 (instead of $150,000). The reason this property's sales price still contains a privatized location value is because in our example the community captures most, but not all, of the property's location value through community land contributions. It's generally good to leave some of a property's location value to existing property owners in order to factor in market fluctuations and to help owners pay for real-estate transaction fees.

65. The property's *periodic* location value—its rent *r*—can be approximated using the property tax-free purchase price of land P and the prevailing interest rate (this formula assumes that the purchase price of land does not contain a speculative component):

$$r = P \times i = \$200,000 \times 3\% = \$6,000$$

If the local community collects 80 percent of this periodic location value, the new property owner would be obligated to pay $4,800 for the first year, or $400 per month.

66. This brings to mind an anecdote: A friend of mine paid for a rent-controlled apartment in San Francisco and left it empty while he lived elsewhere for a year. By retaining his rent-control privilege, he was able to avoid paying a higher rent upon his return to San Francisco and ended up saving money despite having paid for two apartments for an entire year. Laws against such behavior are futile; but if we change the underlying economic incentives, we can avoid the need for such laws altogether. For a good microeconomic perspective on the side effects of rent control, see http://youtube.com/watch?v=wGrirscWV-s

67. For example, the annual cost of emergency room visits and jail stays for the homeless in San Francisco was estimated in 2004 to be approximately $61,000 per person, whereas the cost of providing a homeless person with permanent housing, treatment, and care was estimated at only $16,000. See Angela Alioto, et al. "The San Francisco Plan to Abolish Chronic Homelessness," June 30, 2004, San Francisco Mayor's Office of Housing and Community Development.

68. Economist and Nobel laureate Joseph Stiglitz demonstrated that under certain conditions government spending on public goods will increase the value of land by an equal amount. This effect is also known as the Henry George Theorem, named after the eighteenth-century economist and philosopher Henry George, who popularized this theory. See Richard J. Arnott and Joseph E. Stiglitz, "Aggregate Land Rents, Expenditure on Public Goods, and Optimal City Size," *Quarterly Journal of Economics*, 93 (4) (November 1979), 471–500.

69. Data put together by Dan Sullivan, director of an advocacy organization called Saving Communities, shows how the Housing Unaffordability Index (median 2005 house price divided by median 2007 yearly income) is broadly correlated to the property tax rate for major U.S. cities: The lower the property tax (and by

implication the proportionately lower the land contributions), the higher the Unaffordability Index (the less affordable the housing market).

ILLUSTRATION 12-5: UNAFFORDABILITY INDEX

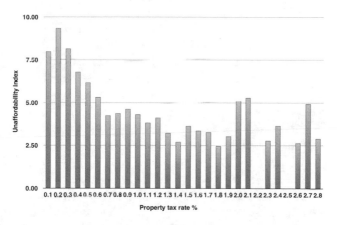

Dan, Sullivan, "Property Tax Rates and Housing Affordability," n.d.

70. In 1993 professor Mason Gaffney of the University of California, Riverside, published a review on the effect of land-value taxes on urban slums in his paper "The Taxable Capacity of Land," in which he identified three types of urban slums and ways to facilitate revitalization.

71. The United States alone lost over 23 million acres of farmland from 1982 to 2007 due to development—an area equal to the entire state of Indiana (U.S. Department of Agriculture, "Summary Report: 2007 National Resources Inventory," 2009).

72. U.S. Department of Agriculture, "Providing Resources for Beginning Farmers and Ranchers," USDA blog, May 8, 2009.

73. National Young Farmers Coalition, "Building a Future with Farmers: Challenges Faced by Young, American Farmers and a National Strategy to Help Them Succeed," November 2011.

74. Cynthia Nickerson et al. "Economic Research Service: Trends in U.S. Farmland Values and Ownership," U.S. Department of Agriculture Economic Information Bulletin 92, February 2012.

75. Is there any data to back up these claims? Although we don't have historical economic data on farmland contributions per se, we do, however, have historical data on property taxes levied on the values of farm buildings and farmland combined. In his 1992 paper "Rising Inequality and Falling Property Tax Rates," Mason Gaffney shows that higher property taxes on farmland benefit farmers, while property tax relief correlates to increased wealth inequality within the agricultural sector (Mason Gaffney, "Rising Inequality and Falling Property Tax Rates," 1992). This increased wealth inequality, according to Gaffney, has potentially disastrous consequences for society: "In the Great Depression (1930–1941), millions of small family farms provided a refuge for the jobless and homeless. Today, that refuge is closed, with explosive social consequences in urban slums."

In his research, Gaffney shows that farmland is used far more productively, and distributed more equitably, if higher property taxes are instituted on farmland. His research also reveals that lower property taxes on farmland allow people and companies to use farmland as a tax shelter and for speculative investment purposes instead of agricultural production. The resulting rise in property prices and the increased appropriation of high-quality farmland by large agribusinesses make it increasingly difficult for farmers to find the best farmland and put it to optimum use. Average farm sizes are increasing as large agribusinesses swallow up land, particularly since property taxes on farmland were lowered in 1930.

ILLUSTRATION 13-4: AVERAGE ACRE PER FARM

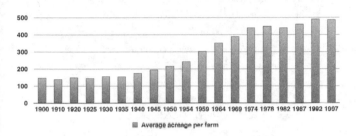

■ Average acreage per farm

Alan Olmstead and Paul Rhode, "Average Acreage per Farm, by Region and State: 1850–1997," in *Historical Statistics of the United States, Earliest Times to the Present: Millennial Edition*, 2006, 225–90

76. For a good summary on the California Wright Act, see Alanna Hartzok, "The Wright Act, California, USA SWOT Analysis," n.d.

77. According to a 2013 report released by the United Nations Conference on Trade and Development (UNCTAD), "The world needs a paradigm shift in agricultural development: from a *green revolution* to an *ecological intensification* approach." The report warns that unless such drastic changes occur, food security may be threatened due to future resource constraints and climate change.

78. WNYC, "Joseph Stiglitz Explains the Price of Inequality," *The Leonard Lopate Show*, June 6, 2012.

79. Mason Gaffney characterized this behavior over forty years ago during the height of the Vietnam War in a seminal paper titled "Benefits of Military Spending: An Inquiry into the Doctrine that National Defense Is a Public Good," in which he analyzed the economic effects of U.S. military engagement in foreign countries and compared them to the effects of urban sprawl: "Urban sprawl means that developers leapfrog over empty land near in and build

far out, pulling social overhead capital along behind them, subsidized by milking the center. Global sprawl means we underutilize resources in the continental United States. Prospectors leapfrog overseas, pulling the United States flag behind them. They find some rich mines out there, just as centrifugal urban land developers find lovely view lots, lakes, and trees. But the whole process is heavily subsidized by milking the heartland." (Mason Gaffney, "Benefits of Military Spending: An Inquiry into the Doctrine that National Defense Is a Public Good," working paper, 1972.)

80. Fred Foldvary, "Peace through Confederal Democracy and Economic Justice," n.d.

81. "A Moral Question," video remix by Sustainable Human. http://vimeo.com/50460060

82. Sweden, for example, has one of the highest standards of living and is now looking to import trash from neighboring countries in order to power its innovative waste-into-energy garbage recycling program—only 4 percent of Sweden's trash ends up in Sweden's landfills (Sophia Jones, "Sweden Wants Your Trash," The Two Way blog, National Public Radio, October 28, 2012). Also, whenever the gifts of nature are shared, a higher standard of living ensues, and populations with higher standards of living tend toward stable population levels. The relationship between population, average per-capita consumption, and the average per-capita efficiency rate with which we conserve nature's gifts can be demonstrated with the following equation:

$$\text{Impact on the ecology} =$$
$$\text{population x consumption x (1–efficiency rate)}$$

The less we use nature's gifts, i.e., the more we share the value of land and reuse sustainable goods that don't pollute the air or tap virgin forests, the higher our efficiency rate (up to, but never greater than, 100 percent). The higher our efficiency rate, the lower our collective negative impact on the ecology. See also

Robert V. Andelson ed., *Commons without Tragedy: Protecting the Environment from Overpopulation—A New Approach* (London: Shepheard-Walwyn, 1991).

83. According to a report by the World Wildlife Fund, humanity's ecological footprint exceeded the Earth's regeneragive capacity by more than 50 percent per year in 2008. (World Wildlife Fund: "Living Planet Report 2012: Biodiversity, Biocapacity, and Better Choices").

84. If we only focus on the political implementation as a means of achieving this new economic paradigm, we miss the point; there have actually been many attempts to legislate the collection of land contributions throughout history (see http://progress.org for a list of historical attempts at reform). Whenever the collection of land contributions has been legislated without an accompanying shift in people's consciousness, so-called *rent seekers* (people seeking to profit from the contributions of others) have found ways to corrupt the original intent and effectiveness of economic reform, usually through the insertion of exemptions and special privileges into the law. This has allowed rent seekers to distort this paradigm to such an extent that its efficiency and justice are no longer recognizable, at which point rent seekers once again argue for the *apparent ineffectiveness* of this paradigm and call for the return to the old ways of profiting from land.

85. There are many ways we can influence the public dialogue in order to help people distinguish house values from land values. When real estate is put up for sale, for example, the listing price could be divided into the house and a land value. Governments could frequently assess land values for economic planning purposes and then release their findings into the public domain. Private-sector companies could even create land-value indices on a parcel-by-parcel basis and then make their indices publicly accessible via the internet. Google, for example, could create a

world-wide land-value index. Measures like these would create greater awareness that "buying a house" not only includes buying a building but also the land underneath it. The next step would then entail helping people realize that the value of land belongs to the community.

86. My dream of sharing has nonetheless stayed with me throughout the years: I remain committed to sharing the resources available to me with the world in the most effective way.

INDEX

Page numbers followed by t indicate table. Page numbers followed by n indicate endnote

ABOUT THE AUTHOR

MARTIN ADAMS is a social innovator, systems thinker, and community organizer. As a child, it pained him to see most people struggling while a few were living in opulence. This inspired in him a lifelong quest to create a fair and sustainable world in collaboration with others. As a young adult, groomed for a career in finance, he walked right past Wall Street and chose instead to dedicate his life to community development. Through his non-profit work, he saw firsthand the extent to which our economic system causes human and ecological strife. Consequently, Adams has devoted himself to the implementation of a new economic paradigm that allows humanity to thrive in harmony with nature. *Land: A New Paradigm for a Thriving World* is the fruit of his years of research into this economic model and stands as an appeal to changemakers worldwide.